P9-CBE-684

Why I Trust the Bible

John MacArthur, Jr.

While this book is designed for the reader's personal enjoyment and profit, it is also intended for group study. A Leader's Guide with Victor Multiuse Transparency Masters is available from your local bookstore or from the publisher.

VICTOR

BOOKS a division of SP Publications, Inc.
WHEATON, ILLINOIS 60187

Offices also in
Whitby, Ontario, Canada
Amersham-on-the-Hill, Bucks, England

Second printing, 1984

Unless otherwise noted, Scripture quotations are from the *King James Version*. Other quotations are from the *New American Standard Bible* (NASB), © 1960, 1962, 1971, 1972, 1973 by the Lockman Foundation, La Habra, California; and *Holy Bible: Revised Standard Version* (RSV), © 1952 by the Division of Christian Education of the National Council of Churches of Christ in the United States.

Recommended Dewey Decimal Classification: 220
 Suggested Subject Headings: BIBLE-AUTHORSHIP, REVELATION, INTERPRETATION, HARMONY

Library of Congress Catalog Card Number: 82-62221
ISBN: 0-88207-389-3

© 1983 by SP Publications, Inc. All rights reserved. Printed in the United States of America. No part of this book may be used or reproduced in any manner whatsoever without written permission except in the case of brief quotations embodied in critical articles and reviews. For information address Victor Books, Wheaton, IL 60187.

Contents

to
Burton Michaelson, my friend,
who has given much of his life
to provide the place where for one-third of my life
I have taught the truths of the Holy Book.

Preface

It is not easy to convince unbelievers that the Bible is the Word of God on the basis of its unity, its scientific and historical accuracy, its miracles, and its archaeological evidence. In a special series spread over a three-week period, I presented such data at a private college in California. I thought the proof was overwhelming, yet to my knowledge not one person became a believer.

Unbelievers cannot accept legitimate proof because they are blind to it. "The natural man receiveth not the things of the Spirit of God: for they are foolishness unto him: neither can he know them, because they are spiritually discerned" (1 Cor. 2:14). Only as the Holy Spirit does His regenerating work—as He opens the mind, tears off the scales of blindness, gives life, and plants the understanding of God's revelation—only then do people believe that the Bible is the Word of God and trust it. I know the Bible is true because the Spirit of God has convinced me of it.

In light of this, I suggest a change in our approach. We have been saying, "Prophecy has been fulfilled. The Bible is scientifically accurate. Miracles were performed. The biblical message of salvation through faith in Jesus Christ results in a revolutionary change in the lives of persons who believe. Because of all of these proofs," we reason, "the Bible is the Word of God." Instead, I propose that we declare, "The Bible is the Word of God; therefore, prophecy has been fulfilled, miracles have taken place, scientific statements are correct, and lives here have been transformed." Confidence in Scripture begins with the work of the Spirit and faith.

I believe the Bible was written by the God of the universe to reveal Himself to humanity. I believe the Bible is the only authoritative and absolutely reliable revelation from God with regard to the origin of man, his deliverance, his salvation, the moral and spiritual standards he is to live by, and his ultimate destiny. I also believe that the Bible is true in every detail, even to the very words in the original manuscripts. God was the author. The Spirit has led me to this supportable confidence.

This book is primarily for you who share this belief and who love the Lord Jesus Christ. I write to stengthen your faith, to help you to have greater confidence in the Bible—to believe it with your whole heart. Then when someone asks, "Why do you believe the Bible?" you will be able to give convincing reasons why you believe it is the Word of God to mankind. "Be ready always to give an answer to every man that asks you a reason of the hope that is in you" (1 Peter 3:15).

If you do not yet believe the Bible, I pray that you too will see what a marvelous Book it is, and that the Holy Spirit will cause you to believe as you read this testimony of its truthfulness.

Introduction

As a pastor who deals with many new believers in the family of God, I have seen the need for a primer on the Bible.

Since the Word of God is the basis of everything, it is essential that we establish its reliability and trustworthiness at the very beginning of a person's Christian life. This book endeavors to do that.

It is not presented as a comprehensive treatise on Scripture or apologetics, but rather as a starting point to strengthen young believers with confidence in God's Word.

1
The
God
Who
Speaks

All mankind is trapped on Planet Earth, captive to time and space and surrounded by an endless universe. Many sense in the deepest parts of their beings that there is an ultimate power or God. And so they try to discover how they can know this Supreme Being. The result is religion, the invention of man in his attempt to find God.

Christianity, however, teaches that we don't find God because God has already found us. He has disclosed Himself to us through His Word. In the Old and New Testaments of Holy Scripture we have the unveiling of God.

The Bible bridges the entire history of the earth. During those long centuries God was always disclosing Himself because it is in His nature to communicate. An artist paints and a singer sings because the ability is in them. God speaks because He desires to make Himself known to His creatures.

Francis Schaeffer, referring to God, wrote, "He is there, and He is not silent."

In the beginning God spoke and the universe was born out of nothing. We read how He spoke to Adam (the first man), to

Abraham, to Moses, and to the prophets. The Jews understood God as a speaking God, and through His messengers they often heard the expression "Thus saith the Lord." In the Books of the Prophets we read it often. "Therefore, say thou unto them, 'Thus saith the Lord of hosts, Turn ye unto Me, saith the Lord of hosts, and I will turn unto you, saith the Lord of hosts'" (Zech. 1:3). Throughout the Book of Ezekiel we read, "And He said unto me," as Jehovah spoke to Ezekiel and called him "Son of man" 91 times.

When Jesus came into the world, He was called the Word. It was an appropriate name for God's revelation in the flesh—the living Word. "In the beginning was the Word, and the Word was with God, and the Word was God. . . . And the Word was made flesh and dwelt among us (and we beheld His glory, the glory as of the only begotten of the Father), full of grace and truth (John 1:1, 14).

What God has spoken does not change. "Forever, O Lord, Thy word is settled in heaven" (Ps. 119:89). Jesus said, "Heaven and earth shall pass away, but My words shall not pass away" (Matt. 24:35). And Peter wrote, "The Word of the Lord endures forever" (1 Peter 1:25).

When God Is Silent

The God who speaks, however, sometimes chooses to remain silent for a time. And when He does, it is in judgment. For example, God freely communicated with King Saul, but Saul's repeated rejection of the Lord and his frequent disobedience finally caught up with him. When Saul called on the Lord, he received no answer. "The Lord answered him not, neither by dreams nor by Urim, nor by prophets" (1 Sam. 28:6).

There came a time when God's patience with Israel was exhausted. He told Jeremiah, the weeping prophet, "Pray not for this people. . . . I will not hear their cry" (Jer. 14:11-12).

We read in the Book of Proverbs that God promised to pour

out His Spirit and to make known His words (Prov. 1:23), but what happens to those who refuse to listen? We are not left to guess.

Because I called, and you refused; I stretched out My hand, and no one paid attention; And you neglected all My counsel, and did not want My reproof; I will even laugh at your calamity; I will mock when your dread comes, When your dread comes like a storm, and your calamity comes on like a whirlwind, When distress and anguish come on you. Then they will call on Me, but I will not answer; They will seek Me diligently, but they shall not find Me (Prov. 1:24-28, NASB).

God freely shares Himself, but if we reject Him—that's it.

God Is Personal

"What is He like—this revealer who speaks?" First, the God who speaks is personal. He calls Himself *I* and addresses those to whom He speaks as *you*. Moses inquired of God as to His name. "And God said unto Moses, *I AM THAT I AM:* and He said, Thus shalt thou say unto the Children of Israel, *I AM* hath sent me unto you" (Ex. 3:14).

I AM indicates personality. God Himself had a name, even as He gave names to others—to Abraham, to Israel, and to the Jews. The name *I AM* stands for a free, purposeful, self-sufficient personality. God is what He wants to be, and He tells us that by His choice of a name.

God is not a floating fog, not an *it.* He is not an aimless, blind force. He is not cosmic energy. God is an almighty, self-existing, self-determining being with mind and will. He is a person!

If you read through the Bible far enough, you find that God is not only personal, but that He is tripersonal. In the opening words of Genesis God said, "Let Us make man in *Our* image, after *Our* likeness" (Gen. 1:26, author's italics). In the Psalms, we have a record of God speaking to God: "The *Lord* said unto My Lord" (Psalm 110:1, author's italics). The New Testament name for God is "Father, Son, and Holy Spirit" (Matt. 28:19, NASB). *God is personal.*

A second characteristic of the revealer God is that He is moral. He is One who is supremely concerned about right and wrong. Morality is a top priority with God. This is wonderfully expressed in His words to Moses: "The Lord God, merciful and gracious, long-suffering, and abundant in goodness and truth, keeping mercy for thousands, forgiving iniquity and transgression and sin, and . . . will by no means clear the guilty" (Ex. 34:6-7).

This may seem contradictory. After speaking of His grace, mercy, and forgiveness, God says that He won't let the guilty go unpunished. This assures us that God is *just*, and that He will not merely say to guilty people, "It's all right. I'll let you off the hook." God does show mercy, but someone has to pay the penalty for sin. The Gospels make it clear that the "Someone" is Jesus Christ.

Getting to Know the Unknown God

A third aspect of the nature of God is that He not only is personal and moral, but He is also the beginning, the maintainer, and the end of all creation. We read in Romans that, "Of Him, and through Him, and to Him are all things" (11:36).

Listen over the shoulder of Paul as he addresses the Athenians on Mars Hill. In effect he said, "Men, as I was coming into your city, I noted all the religious statues you have about. Obviously, you're a pretty religious bunch. I even found one statue dedicated to the 'Unknown God.' Well, I would like you to meet Him. I know Him very well" (Acts 17:23, author's paraphrase).

Paul told his listeners that God was the source of everything: "God that made the world and all things therein, seeing that He is Lord of heaven and earth" (17:24). God also sustains everything: "seeing He giveth to all life, and breath, and all things" (v. 25). "For in Him we live, and move, and have our being" (v. 28). And God is the end, the goal, the purpose of all: "That they should seek the Lord, if haply they might feel after Him, and find Him" (v. 27).

Man's destiny is to seek and to know this God who gives life and who sustains life. The whole purpose of man's existence is fulfilled only when he knows God.

God Is Available

All this is impressive, but it would not mean much if the One who speaks was not available to us. He is available—that is the whole purpose of His self-revelation. He *wants* us to know Him. Because God is a person, He wants to have fellowship with us. The fact that He is moral indicates that He wants to deal with us righteously. The fact that He is the source, the sustainer, and the end of all creation means that our destinies are dependent on our relationship to Him. The fact that He is available to us is the concluding, exciting concept. We can come into a full relationship with the God who speaks—but only through the way that is made so clear to us in His revelation, the Bible. Jesus said, "I am the way, and the truth, and the life; no one comes to the Father but through Me" (John 14:6). Peter declared, "Neither is there salvation in any other; for there is no other name under heaven given among men, whereby we must be saved" (Acts 4:12).

2
How
God
Revealed
Himself

The God who speaks has done so in the Bible—His revelation to us. It is important that we understand this, because much "new revelation" is being claimed today.*

After I had spoken at a seminar, a young woman came to me and asked, "You don't believe there is any more revelation being given today, do you?"

"No," I replied, "I believe the revelation of God is completed."

"Well, I happen to go to a church where we have an apostle," she insisted.

"That's very interesting. Who is he—Peter, James, John, or Paul?"

"Oh, he's not any of those, but he is an apostle."

"How do you know he is an apostle?"

"Because he speaks direct revelation from God."

I blinked. "You mean, when he gets up and talks, it isn't

*For a more comprehensive look at this subject see my book, *The Charismatics*, Zondervan, pp. 15-39.

just a sermon, but it's God speaking through him?"

"That's right. He gives direct revelations every Sunday."

How can we evaluate a claim such as that? What shall we think when we go to a Christian bookstore and pick up a book that describes a revealed vision from God and contradicts or adds to the Bible?

For the answer, we must look to the origin of the claimed message. Did it come from God's voluntary act of love in disclosing Himself, or did it come from the mind of a person who thought he had something that ought to be said?

Did Moses, having nothing better to do one day, suddenly decide that he would record the Creation of the world? "Now, let's see. I wonder how this whole thing came about. It seems to me that. . . ."

That's not how it happened. God told Moses what had occurred, and Moses in obedience, recorded what God revealed to him: "In the beginning God created the heaven and the earth" (Gen. 1:1). This is revelation from God, not supposition from Moses.

Imagine Isaiah sitting down to write, "Therefore the Lord Himself shall give you a sign; Behold, a virgin shall conceive, and bear a son, and shall call His name Immanuel" (Isa. 7:14). I couldn't come up with that, but Isaiah did because it was revealed to him.

Envision Micah saying, "Thou, Bethlehem . . . though thou be little among the thousands of Judah, yet out of thee shall He come forth . . . to be ruler over My people Israel" (Micah 5:2). He couldn't have made such valid prophecy unless it had been revealed to him.

Can you picture David writing in connection with the Crucifixion, "My God, my God, why hast thou forsaken Me?" (Ps. 22:1) and doing it hundreds of years before Jesus was born, if it had not been revealed to him by God?

The great prophecies in the Bible came from God, not from

men. They were God's thoughts, not the speculations of men. (Matt. 16:17; 2 Peter 1:21). Let's think further about God's revelation.

The World of Nature

God has revealed Himself to us in two ways: through *natural revelation* and through *special revelation*. We can't look at the beauties we see in the daytime, or look at the stars of the nighttime without concluding that Someone greater than we are made it all. *Everything* cries out to the existence of God and His work. "For the invisible things of Him from the creation of the world are clearly seen, being understood by the things that are made, even His eternal power and Godhead; so that they are without excuse" (Rom. 1:20).

The world of nature reveals three things. The first is God's power. When we look at the created world, we can only stand in awe of the tremendous power that must have been exerted in its formation. For example, one star, Betelgeuse, is twice the size of the earth's orbit around the sun and is 500 light-years away. At 186,000 miles per second, it takes 500 years for its light to reach the earth and it is on the edge of the universe in which there are billions of stars like it. All were made by God!

Nature also reveals the Godhead. The Greek word for Godhead stresses God's sovereign deity—the fact that He is God. The God who created is sovereign. He runs the show. He is in control of the universe.

Third, nature tells us of God's wrath. We read that the heathen are without excuse in facing God's judgment (Rom. 1:20). It is evident everywhere we look that a curse is on the world—that it is under a moral sentence. The world groans in travail, awaiting redemption (Rom. 8:22).

That briefly is the content of natural revelation.

"Well, it's fuzzy, and hard to understand," you might be

tempted to say. But the Scripture tells us that the fact of God is "clearly seen." Natural revelation is clear. No one can beg off because of ignorance. There is no alibi for atheism, and there is no excuse for agnosticism.

Results of Rejection

If Creation is so clearly the work of a God Creator, why have many missed His conclusion? The difficulty is not in the revelation, but in man.

> Because that, when they knew God, they glorified Him not as God, neither were thankful, but became vain in their imaginations, and their foolish heart was darkened. . . . They . . . changed the glory of the uncorruptible God into an image made like to corruptible man, and to birds, and four-footed beasts, and creeping things (Rom. 1:21-23).

When man deliberately rejected the truth that can be known about God through nature, God gave him up to idolatry (v. 23), to sexual impurity (vv. 24-27), and to a reprobate mind (v. 28). As a result man can't know God on his own, even though he lives in a world that shows God's character, attributes, power, and works. Spiritually, man is dead (Eph. 2:1). A dead man doesn't respond. Man is blind (Eph. 4:18). A blind man can't see the truth no matter how well it is illuminated. The same verse tells us that not only is unregenerate man dead and blind, but he is also ignorant. Dead. Blind. Ignorant. His state is the terrible result of sin!

The Light Inside

Natural revelation is not confined to creation which is external. Natural revelation also comes via conscience. This is internal. "That which may be known of God is manifest in them" (Rom. 1:19). People today, because of what they have on the inside, are conscious that God is. Even Albert Einstein felt he had to believe in a cosmic power. He was convinced that a man who did not believe in a cosmic power as the source of all things was a fool.

A person can deny this, of course. "The fool has said in his heart, 'There is no God'" (Ps. 14:1). Interestingly enough, the word *fool* can also be translated "wicked." Atheists are wicked. That is how they get to be atheists. They have wickedly reduced God to nonexistence in order to entertain their sins without a sense of moral obligation.

In order for the fool to say the word *God*, however, he has to have a concept of God. And if he has a concept of God, that implies that God is. It is impossible to think of something that is not, therefore, he is trying to eliminate something that his very reasoning powers tell him exists. For the fool to work hard enough to eliminate God is testimony that God must be, or the fool wouldn't have to worry about getting rid of Him.

Nature, then, is God's disclosure of Himself in man and in man's environment. Herschel the astronomer said, "The broader the field of science grows, the more manifold and irrefutable become the proofs for the eternal existence of a creative and omnipotent wisdom." Linnaeus, the one-time professor of medicine and botany at Uppsala, declared, "I have seen the footsteps of God." Kepler, the astronomer testified, "In creation I grasped God as if He were in my hands."

A Christian leader of the third century, known for his wisdom, was once asked where he got such wisdom.

The source of all I have learned is in two books. The one is outwardly small, the other is very large. The former has many pages, the latter only two. The pages of the former are white with many black letters on them. One of the pages of the big book is blue, and the other is green. On the blue page there is one big golden letter and many small silver ones. On the green page there are innumerable colored letters in red, white, yellow, blue, and gold.

The small book is the Bible; the large one is nature. These two "books" belong together. Both testify to the revelation of the one living God; their testimonies are in harmony and point to the power, greatness, and love of the Lord of the world.

Sin Became a Barrier

So we have natural revelation given to man through creation and through conscience. Natural revelation was fully effective before the fall of man in the Garden of Eden. Then there was no sin. There was no barrier. Adam and Eve could live with God out of the depths of pure hearts. God didn't need to write to them in the garden, but after the Fall natural revelation was not sufficient. Sin put a barrier between man and a holy God. Someone had to take the punishment for that sin and provide a way to restore man to fellowship with God. God foretold through His prophets (the Old Testament) that such a One would come, and later recorded (the New Testament) how the Son of God came to earth, died, was buried, and rose from the dead. Jesus Christ became the way.

The New Testament makes this clear. Jesus said, "I am the way, the truth, and the life: no man cometh unto the Father, but by Me" (John 14:6). Peter said, "Neither is there salvation in any other: for there is none other name under heaven given among men, whereby we must be saved" (Acts 4:12). Jesus told men that they were condemned because they did not believe on Him (John 3:18). Paul declared to the Philippian jailer, "Believe on the Lord Jesus Christ and thou shalt be saved" (Acts 16:31). Faith in Christ is necessary.

Special Revelation

Special revelation takes up where creation and conscience leave off. Special revelation tells us all we need to know about God—information that was never before understood. It tells us about God's mercy—about His grace—about how sin can be forgiven. It tells about the sacrifice of Christ—about salvation—about the church.

Special revelation gives us specifics. When God speaks, He doesn't mumble. God speaks clearly and to the point, and is precise, even to the very choice of words, and to the verb tenses, even distinguishing between plural and singular.

God's special revelation came progressively. When we read the Book of Genesis, we get part of the revelation of God. It is limited. When we read only the Old Testament, we get only part of the revelation. Scripture is progressive revelation in the sense that it goes from partial to complete, not from error to truth or truth to error.

Some of the Old Testament prophets looked at what they wrote and tried to figure out what it meant. They searched in their own prophecies to determine the fulfillment regarding the Messiah (1 Peter 1:10-12). It was to come later.

Special revelation then, was a process. First God revealed Himself in a small frame, later in larger measure. First revelation was to a man, then to a family, then to a tribe, then to a nation, then to a race, and ultimately to the world.

God Became Man

How has God revealed Himself in special revelation? In three main ways. The first is theophany—the visible appearance of God in some form. We see in the Old Testament that God at times appeared as a man. He and two angels appeared to Abraham as visitors. Abraham greeted the guests and invited them into his house. He asked Sarah to come up with her best culinary delight (Gen. 18:1-8). Imagine—Abraham and his wife fixing a meal to entertain God and two angels! In this instance, God assumed human form to appear to man.

There were other ways God revealed Himself in visible form. In the account of Moses and the burning bush (Ex. 3),

God appeared as the Shekinah Glory in the Tabernacle (Ex. 33—40). Jacob wrestled with an "angel"—God (Gen. 32:24-32). Theologians call this a Christophany—a pre-incarnate appearance of Christ.

The greatest theophany of all, in a sense, concerns the coming of the Lord Jesus Christ in human form to walk on earth and to dwell with men. God is not a man, as the Bible clearly teaches. "God is Spirit" (John 4:24), but He has chosen to reveal Himself in human form, and that most perfectly in Christ.

Note that in each of these cases, God's special revelation accomplished a specific purpose. God had a specific message for Abraham, for Moses, and for the others. Each had no doubt about what God was trying to communicate.

When God wanted to communicate specifically, it was not necessary for Him to appear in person. He also spoke through the mouth of a prophet. The man of God would open his mouth and say, "Thus saith the Lord." God would take control of his mind and mouth. In fact, sometimes in studying the Prophets it is impossible to isolate God from the prophet speaking.

Take Deuteronomy 18:18, for example: "I will raise them up a Prophet from among their brethren, like unto thee, and will put My words in his mouth; and he shall speak unto them all that I shall command him." Here is a prophecy concerning Christ, but it also pictures a human prophet.

The commission of Jeremiah as a prophet is another example: "Then the Lord put forth His hand, and touched my mouth. And the Lord said unto me, Behold, I have put My words in thy mouth" (Jer. 1:9). When Jeremiah opened his mouth, God's Word came out.

It is also amazing to notice other ways God put His messages across. Sometimes He communicated by the casting of lots. God wanted Jonah to take a short ride in a long fish, and God wanted to make sure it would happen that way. So the pagan sailors on board the sinking ship cast lots, and the lot fell on Jonah. God made sure Jonah got the short stick.

Another fascinating way God communicated to His people was through use of the Urim and the Thummim, though no one today is quite clear as to their exact identification. All we know is that they fit into the breastplate of the high priest—perhaps they were beautiful stones or jewelry (Lev. 8:8). Somehow they were used to tell the will of God (Ez. 2:63; 1 Sam. 28:6).

God also communicated through dreams, as in the case of Jacob (Gen. 28:12-15), Joseph (37:5-10), the butler and baker (40:5-23), and Pharaoh (41:1-44).

Another very common way for God to communicate was through visions. Daniel had both dreams and visions to learn the will and purposes of God.

At times God communicated by speaking audibly. For example, God said to Abraham, "Get thee out of thy country, and from thy kindred, and from thy father's house, unto a land that I will show thee" (Gen. 12:1).

Think of the Apostle Paul on his way to Damascus. All of a sudden the Lord talked right out of heaven to him. What a fantastic concept. God could send His voice across the sky, from heaven to communicate orally.

The Means of a Miracle
In addition to communicating through nature and prophecy, God spoke through miracles. Simply defined, a miracle is an extraordinary event manifesting God's intervention so that He may specially reveal Himself.

Jesus verified His teaching with miracles that people might know He was God. The entire Gospel of John supports this. Jesus healed the lame man as easily as He forgave the man's sins (Mark 2:1-12). Only God could do that. This miracle demonstrated and authenticated the reality of the deity of Christ.

God used miracles to attest the truth of His preaching. Elijah, for example, could announce what God had said, and someone could say, "How do we know you're telling the truth?" When Elijah raised somebody from the dead, it would bring a response of confidence that God was at work.

Peter preached the Gospel. Then he demonstrated divine power by healing the sick. That made people say, "This man must really be from God."

We see, in the New Testament accounts especially, that God accompanied His Word with signs in order that men might know that it was His Word. In 2 Corinthians 12:12 we read about signs and wonders and the mighty deeds of the apostles that were used to certify the Word.

Any miracle testifies that God exists. It is one way God lets us know, "I am here, and I have something to say."

We should note that it is no problem for God to perform a miracle. He made the world, didn't He? For God, a miracle is like sticking His finger into a pond and making waves. And when God does a miracle, it doesn't create havoc in nature during the remaining time till Jesus comes. It is self-contained. For example, Jesus stood at the tomb and said, "Lazarus, come forth," and Lazarus came out and took off the grave clothes. But later he died again (John 11:43).

In his book *The Life of Jesus,* Ernest Renan indicates that he regards Bible miracles as legends. The raising of Lazarus was pure hypothesis. Lazarus was only spoken of as if he had been raised from the dead. Renan further called it a tradition. He is convinced that if we know out of what inaccuracies, what incoherent fables the gossip of an Eastern city is made up, we cannot regard it as impossible that a rumor of this kind was spread abroad. At times he infers that the family at Bethany was guilty of some indiscretion (World Publishing Co.).

Apparently Renan was saying that the family so wanted people to believe in the power of Christ, that Lazarus faked being dead and set up a phony resurrection. He suggests that Lazarus may have had himself placed in the tomb and then had Mary and Martha put on an act to go along with the ruse.

For All to See

Miracles do stand—and so do all the other means through which God has chosen to reveal Himself. They are recorded for us in the Bible, the embodiment of God's self-disclosure.

Jesus never healed anyone, Renan said. He only aided sick people by His gentleness so that they felt better. But His followers considered these actions miracles. At the Sea of Galilee, according to Renan, Jesus was not walking on water but was stepping on a very heavy growth of lily pads.

How did the feeding of the 5,000 occur? Renan declared that a large quantity of food was stored in a nearby cave. Jesus knew about it and ordered His disciples to sneak it out.

It takes more faith to believe Renan's explanations than it does to accept the Bible record as it stands.

Isaiah, in his day, even with all God said to the prophets, wanted more: "Verily Thou art a God that hidest Thyself. . . . Oh that Thou would rend the heavens, that Thou would come down" (Isa. 45:15; 64:1). And He did:

God, who at sundry times and in diverse manners spoke in time past unto the fathers by the prophets, hath in these last days spoken unto us by His Son, whom He hath appointed heir of all things, by whom also He made the world; Who being the brightness of His glory, and the express image of His person, and upholding all things by the Word of His power, when He had by Himself purged our sins, sat down on the right hand of the Majesty on high (Heb. 1:1-3).

This becomes clear in the next aspect of our study.

3
God's Inspired Word

Revelation and inspiration are not the same. Revelation is the message and inspiration was the primary method of delivering that message to mankind. Inspiration is the act of the Holy Spirit in revealing to human writers the message that God intended to comprise the Old and New Testaments.

In order to make our definition clear, let us look at what inspiration is *not*. First, *inspiration is not a high level of human achievement*. Think of Homer's *Odyssey*, Mohammed's *Koran*, Dante's *Divine Comedy*, or Shakespeare's tragedies. Some people say that the Bible is inspired in the same way that those great works of literature were inspired. In other words, the Bible, they say, is just the product of genius—it is the result of natural inspiration; therefore, the Bible has errors in it—fallible material that we can't believe. They acknowledge that the Bible has high ethics and morals in certain parts and great insights into humanity, but it is, after all, only an achievement on the same level as other great writings.

We have problems with that view because it is saying that God didn't write this Book—that smart men did. Would smart men write a book that condemns men to hell? Would smart men write a book that provides no human means of salvation apart from the perfect sacrifice of Jesus Christ? No! Man writes books that exalt himself. He doesn't write books to damn himself. The Bible cannot be simply the product of human achievement.

Second, *inspiration is not only in the thoughts of the writers*. Some say that instead of giving the writers specific words, God supplied only general ideas and the choice of vocabulary was theirs. It is as if God zapped Paul with a thought about what a nice thing love is, and then the apostle sat down and wrote 1 Corinthians 13. According to this belief, men were free to say what they wanted and that is why, though the overall truths are divine, mistakes appear in the Bible.

That view doesn't square with what the Bible teaches. Paul wrote, "We speak, not in the words which man's wisdom teaches, but which the Holy Spirit teaches" (1 Cor. 2:13). The "words" are the words of the Spirit, Paul declared. Inspiration was not only in concepts and in thoughts, but in words as well.

Jesus said, "I have given unto them the words which Thou gavest Me" (John 17:8). Some 3,808 times in the Old Testament, expressions such as "Thus saith the Lord," "The Word of the Lord," and "The Word of God" appear. These hardly express wordless concepts. God communicates in words.

Take the case of Moses. When Moses tried to excuse himself from God's call on the basis of a speech problem, God didn't say, "I will inspire your thoughts." Rather, He promised, "I will be with thy mouth . . . and will teach you what ye shall do" (Ex. 4:15). God didn't inspire thoughts; He inspired words.

That is why 40 years later Moses was so insistent on giving verbatim instructions to the people of Israel: "Ye shall not add unto the word which I command you, neither shall ye diminish ought from it, that ye may keep the commandments of the

Lord your God which I command you" (Deut. 4:2). "Don't add to the word and don't take away from the word," Moses was saying. Why? "Because God gave me these specific words for you."

From the Holy Spirit

One of the greatest arguments against "thought inspiration" is found in 1 Peter where we read this about the work of the Old Testament prophets in telling of salvation:

> Of which salvation the prophets have enquired and searched diligently, who prophesied of the grace that should come unto you: Searching what, or what manner of time the Spirit of Christ which was in them did signify, when it testified beforehand the sufferings of Christ, and the glory that should follow (1 Peter 1:10-11).

The Spirit gave prophecies to the writers who wrote them down, read them, and tried to figure out what they meant.

"Well," you say, "what's so amazing about that?"

It is the fact that they received words without understanding. They recorded what they were told, but they didn't fully understand what they were writing. God didn't give them thoughts that they then expressed in their own words. God gave them the words. This is why we view as important the pronouns, prepositions, and conjunctions which may seem minimal. Jesus said, "Heaven and earth shall pass away, but My words shall not pass away" (Matt. 24:35).

The exchange between Peter and Christ supports the word-inspiration idea. When Peter said, "Thou art the Christ, the Son of the living God," Jesus answered, "Flesh and blood hath not revealed it unto thee, but My Father which is in heaven" (Matt. 16:16-17). Peter was speaking right off the top of his head what God was revealing in his mind. God gave him specific words, not just thoughts.

One writer has said, "Thoughts are wedded to words as soul

to body." As far as thoughts being inspired apart from the words which give them expression, you might as well talk about a tune without notes or a sum without figures. We cannot have geology without rocks, or anthropology without men. We cannot have a melody without music, nor can we have a divine record of God without words. Thoughts are carried by words, and God revealed His thoughts in words. We call that *verbal inspiration*.

Goose-bump Theology

There is a third thing that inspiration is not. *Inspiration is not the act of God on the reader.* There are some who teach what we could call existential inspiration, which means that the only part of the Bible that is inspired is what zaps you. You read along and you get "goose bumps," meaning that a particular word or passage is inspired *to you*. It becomes God's Word when it hits you. If you get ecstatic and emotional, convicted or confronted, then it is God's Word to you, but if you sit there unresponsively, it is not the Word of God. It is not generally authoritative.

There are those who say there are myths in Scripture and try to "demythologize" the Bible. They want to eliminate what they think is untrue. With this reasoning or approach they may edit out the preexistence of Christ, the virgin birth, the deity of Christ, the miracles, the substitutionary death, the Lord's resurrection, His ascension, His return, and His coming judgment. All of that, they may maintain, is historically false. To reject the historical character of Scripture and maintain that it can still say something spiritually meaningful and from God doesn't make sense. If the Bible lies from beginning to end historically, why should we believe its spiritual message? If the Book is lying where it is verifiable in history, why should we believe it in its spiritual content where we can't easily verify it? It seems to me that if God wanted us to trust the spiritual character of the Bible, He would make sure that the historical character of the Bible would be trustworthy.

Jesus said, "Thy word is truth" (John 17:17). Inspiration is not the inspiration of the reader.

To conclude what inspiration is not: *Inspiration is not mechanical dictation.* The Bible writers were not robots, writing in a semicomatose state, cranking it all out with no involvement of their minds.

It is true that God could have used dictation to give us the truth—He didn't have to use men. God could have spoken His Word into existence and dropped it on us like revelatory rain. But we know that He didn't do it that way because when we open the Bible, we find personality. Every book has a different character. Each author has a unique style. There are variations in language and vocabulary. And when we read the various books of the Bible, we can feel the emotions the writers were experiencing at the time.

At Work in the Writer

But how can the Bible be the Word of God and at the same time, for example, the words of Paul? God formed the personality of the writer. God made Paul into the man He wanted him to be. God controlled his heredity and his environment. When the writer reached the point that God desired and intended, God directed and controlled the free and willing choice of the man so that he wrote down the very words of God. God literally selected the words out of each author's own life, out of his personality, his vocabulary, and his emotions. The words were man's words, but that man's life had been so framed by God that they were God's words as well. So we can say that Paul wrote Romans, and we can say God wrote it and be correct in both statements.

David testified, "The Spirit of the Lord spoke by me, and His word was in my tongue" (2 Sam. 23:2). It came out as

God's Word. Thrilling! Holy men of God were moved along by the Holy Spirit (2 Peter 1:21). They were authors, not secretaries. They wrote out of their personalities. We read Jeremiah, the weeping prophet, and we can feel his emotion. We read about the fires of judgment expressed by Amos, and we can almost experience it. Personality comes through every part of Scripture.

To sum up, inspiration is not a high level of human achievement; it is not confined to thoughts alone; it is not the act of God on the reader; and it is not mechanical dictation.

To understand the real meaning of inspiration, we need to look at a key passage on the subject. "All Scripture is given by inspiration of God" (2 Tim. 3:16). That could be translated, "All Scripture is God-breathed" because the Greek word *theopneustos* comes from the words *God* and *breath*. The expression means that which comes out of God's mouth—His Word.

As we study the doctrine of inspiration, we discover that this is the method by which God has acted. Earlier we saw that natural revelation came about by the breath of God: "By the word of the Lord were the heavens made; and all the host of them by the breath of His mouth" (Psalms 33:6). God breathed the universe into existence. Then God breathed the Bible into existence. Special revelation comes about in the same way natural revelation did—by the breath of God. Whatever the Scriptures say, God said. Sometimes *the Scripture* is used in place of *God*. The *Scriptures say*, "In thee shall all the nations be blessed" (Gal. 3:8). And, "But the *Scripture hath concluded* all under sin, that the promise by faith of Jesus Christ might be given to them that believe" (Gal. 3:22, author's italics). Here the Bible speaks and acts as the voice of God.

We find the same in the Old Testament. In Exodus we read that God said to Pharaoh, "And in very deed for this cause have I raised thee up, for to show in thee My power; and that

My name may be declared throughout all the earth" (9:16). That is God speaking. Paul referred to this conversation in Romans 9:17, but he wrote, "For the *Scripture saith* unto Pharaoh, Even for this same purpose have I raised thee up" (author's italics). When the Scripture speaks, God speaks. When God speaks, the Scripture speaks. In every sense, when you pick up the Word and read it, you are hearing God's voice. This is exciting. God is the author of what Scripture records. The Bible is the very Word of God.

From Him through Them to Us
The Bible writers in both the Old and New Testaments were commissioned to write the revelation of God in God's own words. Isaiah had a vision of the Lord sitting on His throne. He wrote, "I heard the voice of the Lord, saying, 'Whom shall I send, and who will go for us?'" (Isa. 6:8) Isaiah recorded the words of God.

The Prophet Jeremiah wrote, "Then the word of the Lord came unto me saying, 'Before I formed thee in the belly I knew thee; and before thou camest forth out of the womb I sanctified thee, and I ordained thee a prophet unto the nations'" (Jer. 1:4-5). "Then the Lord put forth His hand, and touched my mouth. And the Lord said unto me, 'Behold I have put My words in thy mouth'" (v. 9). What would be the results? "Because ye speak this word, behold, I will make My words in thy mouth fire, and this people wood, and it shall devour them" (5:14). That is vivid!

Ezekiel testified time after time that he spoke the words God had given him. God said to His prophet, "Son of man, all My words that I shall speak unto thee receive in thine heart, and hear with thine ears. And go, get thee to them of the captivity, unto the children of thy people, and speak unto them, and tell them, 'Thus saith the Lord God'" (Ez. 3:10-11). And he did.

Paul wrote to the Galatians that it was God who gave him his message: "But when He who had set me apart, *even* from my mother's womb, and called me through His grace, was pleased to reveal His Son in me, that I might preach Him among the Gentiles, I did not immediately consult with flesh and blood" (Gal. 1:15-16, NASB). Paul did not get his message from his fellow apostles—it came directly from God.

Think of John the disciple. Is the Book of Revelation something he conceived? Never. "I was in the Spirit on the Lord's Day, and heard behind me a great voice, as of a trumpet, saying . . . 'What thou seest, write in a book, and send it unto the seven churches'" (Rev. 1:10-11).

All these Bible writers—and the others as well—gave clear-cut evidence that what they wrote was from God; it was the breath of God. This is one essential factor of inspiration.

Some, Most, or All?

But now the question arises, "How much of Scripture is God-breathed?" Let's return to 2 Timothy 3:16 and check out another Greek word: "*All* Scripture is given by inspiration of God." The word *all—pasa* in the Greek—can be translated "every." So we see that *all* Scripture and every Scripture is inspired.

Consider an analogy in the form of a statement: All ducks waddle. Does that mean that only ducks of the past waddle? No. Ducks still waddle today. What about future ducks? Future ducks will also waddle. In other words, in whatever period of history ducks live, ducks waddle.

Here is the point: To say Scripture is God-breathed means *all* Scripture, regardless of when it was written, is God-breathed.

This unity of the Scripture as a body of truth was taught by the Lord Jesus when He said, "Scripture cannot be broken"

(John 10:35). All Scripture is pure and authentic. None can be violated. The Lord meant *all* that had been written, *all* that was being written, and *all* that would be written. All Scripture are the holy writings of God.

There is a third Greek word we need to examine. It is *graphe* from which we get the term graphite—the lead that goes into a pencil. *Graphe*, then, is writing. All *writing*—all Scripture. Paul wrote to Timothy, "And how from childhood you have been acquainted with the sacred writings which are able to instruct you for salvation through faith in Christ Jesus" (2 Tim. 3:15, RSV). When we talk about writing being inspired, we refer to the Scriptures only—the "sacred writings."

There is a point here that we might miss. What is it that is inspired? The writers? No, the writings. Paul was not inspired, but the Book of Romans that he wrote was inspired. And that is true of the other letters that he wrote as well. They were inspired, but not the author. "All *Scripture*," said Paul.

The Bible never says that Moses was inspired, or David, or Paul—not the men, but the message. That is why a man could write an inspired message at one period in his life and perhaps no other during the remainder of his life.

Despite that teaching, however, we have people around today who want to remove this verse or some other verse or passage from Scripture. They want to decide what stays and what goes. The principle they follow is something they call the "spirit of Jesus." Whatever in the Bible fits the spirit of Jesus, they accept. Whatever doesn't fit the spirit of Jesus, they reject.

Perhaps they are reading in the New Testament and come across the account of our Lord's cleansing of the temple. They want to deny that this incident took place, rationalizing that it is not really a part of Scripture because it isn't in the meek and loving spirit of Jesus. Their concept of Jesus is a sort of Casper

Milquetoast character who is so meek and gentle that He has
no sense of judgment or justice. They make Jesus what they
wish, and they throw out of Scripture anything that doesn't
conform to their "fantasy Jesus."

But Jesus said, "For truly I say to you, until heaven and
earth pass away, not the smallest letter or stroke shall pass
away from the Law, until all is accomplished" (Matt. 5:18,
NASB). The Greek words refer to a very small mark, similar in
size to our punctuation marks, placed under a word like a dot
or a comma. Not one shall be removed. It is not to be
touched—it is that serious. Yet we have people going through
the Bible cutting out whole passages.

Warnings in the Word

Jesus warns, "Whoever then relaxes one of the least of these
commandments and teaches men so, shall be called least in the
kingdom of heaven" (Matt. 5:19, RSV). God doesn't want anyone tampering with His words.

What would it take to change the Word of God? "It is easier
for heaven and earth to pass away than for one stroke of a
letter of the Law to fail" (Luke 16:17, NASB). It is easier for the
entire universe to fold up than for the smallest mark in the
Bible to be altered. God's Word is eternal!

This doesn't mean that men won't tamper with it. Jesus told
the Pharisees that they had "invalidated" the Word of God by
their tradition which they had handed down (Mark 7:13,
NASB). They had destroyed the effectiveness of Scripture by
their additions and misinterpretations. In setting aside a part,
they were in effect, casting aside the whole, for the Bible is a
unit that is not meant to be broken.

Thy word is true from the beginning; and every one of Thy
righteous judgments endures for ever (Ps. 119:160). Another
important passage bears on this matter: "But know this first of
all, that no prophecy of Scripture is a matter of one's own

interpretation, for no prophecy was ever made by an act of human will, but men moved by the Holy Spirit spoke from God" (2 Peter 1:20-21, NASB). This refers to origin. Scripture did not originate privately. It didn't come out of a man's mind, but by men carried along by the Holy Spirit.

"But this is talking only about prophecy," someone may point out.

Yes, but prophecy isn't only prediction. Genesis, Exodus, Leviticus, Numbers, and Deuteronomy are prophecies. These books, called the Pentateuch, were written by Moses, and Moses was a prophet.

There are predictions as to the coming Messiah in them, but basically those books are history. Prophecy doesn't have to be predictive. Prophecy means "speaking," or "telling forth." It is a communication from God, and all communication from God came, not by the will of man, but by men used as they were borne along by the Holy Spirit.

We see that inspiration is God's revelation communicated to us through writers who used their own minds and their own words. God had so arranged their lives, their thoughts, and their vocabularies that the words they chose were the words that God determined from eternity past that they would use to write His truth.

"That's a miracle!" you exclaim.

Theologians call it the plenary verbal inspiration of Scripture. Plenary means all. Nothing is missing. Verbal means word. So every word in the Bible is God-breathed.

Now what logically follows from that definition? First, the Bible is *infallible*. It speaks only the truth. If God wrote it, it has to be. "The Law of the Lord is perfect" (Ps. 19:7).

No Mistakes

In addition to being perfect, the Bible is also *inerrant* in the original manuscripts—no mistakes. It is true that as the Bible has come down to us through the generations of man, there may be slight variations in the manuscripts. These are apparent and generally known to us. But basically, we can look at the totality of the Word of God and say, This is, as it was in the original language, the Word of God. Even as He upholds the world by the Word of His power, so He upholds the Bible in an infallible state.

That should caution us again about tampering with the Word of God. We read, "Do not add to His words lest He reprove you, and you be proved a liar" (Prov. 30:6, NASB). When anyone wants to add a new revelation or claim new inspiration, he falls into the category of those described in Revelation 22:

> I warn every one who hears the words of the prophecy of this book: if any one adds to them, God will add to him the plagues described in this book, and if any one takes away from the words of the book of this prophecy, God will take away his share in the tree of life and in the holy city, which are described in this book (vv. 18-19, RSV).

No More Needed

In addition to being infallible and inerrant, Scripture is also _complete_. The Bible is all that we need to have a right relationship with God. We don't need a vision. We don't need a new revelation or a voice from heaven. The Scriptures are "the faith which was once for all delivered to the saints" (Jude 3, RSV).

The New Testament books demanded (for their authentication) authorship by an apostle or someone close to an apostle. We read that the apostles were the foundation of the church (Eph. 2:20). In this 20th century the foundation is not being relaid. There are no more apostles; therefore, there are no more revelations. Today we enjoy the illumination of Scripture by the Holy Spirit, not by contemporary inspiration.

The Word of God is also *authoritative*. When it speaks, we had better respond. "Hear, O heavens, and give ear, O earth; for the LORD has spoken" (Isa. 1:2, RSV). That says it all. This is God's voice recorded in Scripture, and we'd better hear it.

The Bible is *sufficient.* Because the Word of God is the breath of God, we don't need anything more. Go back again to that basic text, "All Scripture is inspired by God and profitable for teaching, for reproof, for correction, for training in righteousness; that the man of God may be adequate, equipped for every good work" (2 Tim. 3:16-17, NASB). The *King James Version* says, "That the man of God may be perfect." Is there anything needed beyond perfection? Is anything missing? When we say the Bible is sufficient, we mean nothing is missing. Paul wrote that Timothy from childhood had known the sacred writings which were able to give him the wisdom that leads to salvation through faith which is in Christ Jesus (2 Tim. 3:15, NASB). The Bible is all anyone needs to find salvation and to become mature in Christ.

When a person comes along to trouble you and says, "Oh, you need this spiritual or mystical experience," don't believe it. The Spirit of God acting through the Word of God is sufficient to make you fully mature in Christ.

We have said that the Bible is infallible, inerrant, complete, authoritative, and sufficient. The Bible is also *effective*. "For the word of God is living and active and sharper than any two-edged sword, and piercing as far as the division of soul and spirit, of both joints and marrow, and able to judge the thoughts and intentions of the heart" (Heb. 4:12, NASB). God said, "So shall My Word be which goes forth from My mouth; it shall not return to Me empty, without accomplishing what I desire, and without succeeding *in the matter* for which I sent it" (Isa. 55:11, NASB). And Paul said to the Thessalonians, "For our Gospel did not come to you in word only, but also in power and in the Holy Spirit and with full conviction" (1 Thes. 1:5, NASB).

The Word of God is effective—all believers have experienced this in their lives. The Bible is a powerful book. It tears me up and it puts me back together again. Take the Word of God and the Spirit of God and we have dynamite.

One of the reasons I know that God wrote the Bible is that it tells me things about myself that only He and I know, and usually at a depth I didn't understand before. And then through the Word He rearranges me to be what He wants me to be.

Beloved, we are to stand faithfully and carefully on this inspired Word of God which is infallible, inerrant, complete, authoritative, sufficient, and effective. But there are many people who don't. Our Lord told us why: "He that is of God hears God's words: ye therefore hear them not, because ye are not of God" (John 8:47).

One way to tell a saved person from an unsaved one is that one listens to the Word of God and the other doesn't. Are you listening?

4
What the Bible Says about Itself

Imagine that you are in a court of law and that the Bible is on trial. You are counsel for the defense. What witnesses can you call to give testimony to the truthfulness, and the authoritative infallibility of the Bible?

I think I would appeal to at least three different sources. The first would be the Bible writers themselves, the human instruments through which the revelation was given. Two Bible writers were kings. Two were priests. One was a physician. Two were fishermen. Two were shepherds. Paul was a Pharisee and a theologian. Daniel was a statesman. Matthew was a tax collector. Joshua was a soldier. Ezra was a scribe. Nehemiah was a butler. The list goes on.

As we begin to take the testimony of the 40 or more who wrote over a period of 1,600 years, we discern a common air of infallibility, beginning with Moses who wrote the Pentateuch, and ending with the Apostle John who wrote Revelation. With a few exceptions they were the simplest kind of men, without formal education, yet these fishermen, farmers, shepherds, and a tax collector were confident that they were setting down the Word of God.

That is astounding. Several thousand times in the Bible, in one way or another, these men who wrote the Bible claimed to be writing the Word of God.

If I were to sit down and write something and announce, "This is the revelation of God," people would say, "Who do you think you are?" I would be very self-conscious about making any declaration that what I had written was God's Word—but not the Bible writers. There is no self-consciousness, no effort to convince us that they were really relating the Word of God. They made the claim, and that settled it.

No Apologies

You'll not find in the Bible any statement such as these: "Friends, this may sound ridiculous, but this is the Word of God. . . . You may find this very hard to believe, but God actually gave me these words. . . . I know you're going to find this difficult to believe, but . . . ."

Recall how Peter was in Jerusalem preaching and firing off all kinds of wonderful messages when He was hauled before the Sanhedrin for trial. Did he say, "Now I realize that we are ignorant and unlearned Galileans, and you're not going to believe this, but can I speak to you from God?"

Of course not. There was an air of authority about his preaching, an infallibility to his witnessing. He could boldly declare, "Neither is there salvation in any other: for there is none other name under heaven given among men, whereby we must be saved" (Acts 4:12).

All the Bible writers wrote with the same authority. Though they lived in different times and circumstances, they wove a perfect, never-contradictory theme which is the Word of God.

These writers touched on many areas. The Bible contains history that can be verified. The Bible contains science, and that science is right, "He . . . hangeth the earth upon nothing" (Job 26:7). The Bible talks about medicine and gives laws of health. Doctors today verify that the Bible has information that can contribute to a healthy life. There is commentary on ethics, and there is practical wisdom essential to a happy life.

Sometimes it takes scientists a long time to catch up with what the Bible has been saying all along. It wasn't until the 16th century that William Harvey discovered the workings of the circulatory system in the human body. Yet the first book in the Bible declares that the life of the flesh is in the blood (Gen. 9:4).

Herbert Spencer, who died in 1903, announced that everything in the universe fits into five categories—time, force, action, space, and matter. Everybody said, "Wonderful." But Moses wrote in the first verse of the Bible, "In the beginning [time] God [force] created [action] the heaven [space] and the earth [matter]" (Gen. 1:1).

Then there is prophecy. For example, the Bible predicted that Babylon, the greatest city of the ancient world, would be destroyed. At the time, that statement was scorned as irresponsible—it was comparable to saying that the Boy Scouts would demolish New York. It couldn't happen. Yet Babylon was destroyed just as the Bible said. Such examples are numerous.

The only reasonable source for such vast amounts of information was certainly outside the writers. If God didn't write the Bible, then who did? Mere men acting on their own could never have done it.

His Word

What are the claims of Bible writers? Let's call the Old Testament authors into our courtroom and ask them. They refer to their writings as the very words of God 3,808 times. Once would be enough, but 3,808 times is more than sufficient. This amount of testimony builds a substantial case.

From Psalms 19 and 119, for example, come such statements as "The Law of the Lord is perfect. . . . I hope in Thy Word. . . . Thy Word is very pure. . . . Thy Law is truth. . . . All Thy commandments are truth. . . . Every one of Thy righteous judgments endureth forever. . . . My tongue shall speak of Thy Word; for all Thy commandments are righteousness."

The Prophet Amos testified, "Surely the Lord God will do nothing, but He revealeth His secret unto His servants the prophets" (3:7). God told His prophets what He was going to do, and the testimony of these Old Testament writers is that God breathed the very words of the Book.

What about the New Testament writers? Did they believe what the Old Testament writers believed? At least 320 quotations in the New Testament come directly out of the Old Testament. Check, for example, the words of Paul: "For whatsoever things were written aforetime [the Old Testament] were written for our learning, that we through patience and comfort of the Scriptures might have hope" (Rom. 15:4). Paul considered the Old Testament writings Scripture.

Peter said that holy men of God wrote as they were borne along by the Holy Spirit (2 Peter 1:21). Peter believed that the Old Testament was inspired. The writer of Hebrews said that "God, who at sundry times and in divers manners spoke in time past unto the fathers by the prophets" (Heb. 1:1). That writer believed the Old Testament was the Word of God. James, in a passage describing the authority of the Old Testament writings, called them *Scripture* (James 4:5).

The Witness of Acts

There are many illustrations of how New Testament writers referred to the Old Testament, and indicated their belief that God wrote it. Consider these in the Book of Acts.

In his sermon Peter said, "Men and brethren, this Scripture

must needs have been fulfilled, which the Holy Spirit by the mouth of David spoke before concerning Judas, which was guide to them that took Jesus" (Acts 1:16). This is a conclusive statement that the Old Testament was equally inspired by the Holy Spirit. In fact, Peter was saying that the Holy Spirit used David's mouth to speak. This is a New Testament writer's view of the Old Testament inspiration.

In Acts 4:25 is another example. "Who by the mouth of Thy servant David hast said." A better translation would be, "Who, by the Holy Spirit through the mouth of Thy servant David, hast said." Here is a quotation from the Old Testament that is not only assigned to David but also to the Holy Spirit. So again we find that the Christians in the early church believed that what came through David's mouth was equally the Word of God.

These are only two illustrations from Acts underscoring the fact that the New Testament writers believed that the words of the prophets in the Old Testament Scriptures were in fact the words of the Holy Spirit. There are many other examples that we could cite.

A further element concerns us. Do New Testament writers ever say that other New Testament writers are inspired? Is there any testimony from New Testament writers about other New Testament writers? The Book of 1 Timothy sets us off on an exciting investigation: "For the Scripture saith, Thou shalt not muzzle the ox that treadeth out the corn" (5:18). We read that principle in Deuteronomy 25:4. Paul quotes that and calls it Scripture, and then goes on to say, "The laborer is worthy of his reward," which are the words of the Lord Jesus recorded in Luke 10:7. Paul is saying that both the Old Testament and the New Testament are Scripture. So here is a New Testament writer corroborating the New Testament as Scripture.

The Book of 2 Peter provides further support:
And account that the long-suffering of our Lord is salva-

tion; even as our beloved brother Paul also according to the wisdom given unto him hath written unto you; as also in all his epistles, speaking in them of these things; in which are some things hard to be understood, which they that are unlearned and unstable wrest, as they do also the other Scriptures, unto their own destruction (3:15-16).

Peter was saying, "I'm telling you what our beloved Paul said." In doing that, Peter declared that all the Epistles of Paul are Scripture and do what the other Scriptures do—instruct us in the ways of God. What Paul wrote was as much the Word of God as the Old Testament. This is one of the great statements on New Testament inspiration. It covers Romans, 1 and 2 Corinthians, Galatians, Ephesians, Philippians, Colossians, 1 and 2 Thessalonians, 1 and 2 Timothy, Titus, and Philemon.

The Last Word
What about John and the Book of Revelation? At the beginning of each message to the seven churches John testifies, "These things saith He," referring to the Lord Jesus. He also wrote, "Let him hear what the Spirit saith." John was saying that all of the Revelation was coming from Jesus Christ through him, and that the whole is the message of the Holy Spirit. Throughout the Revelation he included such expressions as "These are the true sayings of God" (19:9), and "These words are true and faithful" (21:5).

Taken together, we have inspiration established for the Gospels, for the Epistles, and for the Book of Revelation. The testimony of the New Testament writers is that they wrote the Word of God.

In addition to the testimony of the writers themselves, we have a second witness—the Lord Jesus Christ. He had a number of vital things to say about His view of Scripture. He acknowledged that He was the theme of all Scripture. Jesus said to the Jewish leaders, "You search the Scriptures, because you think that in them you have eternal life; and it is they that bear witness to Me" (John 5:39, RSV).

Not only did Christ teach that He was the theme of all Scripture, but He also said that He came to fulfill all Scripture. He said, "Think not that I am come to destroy the Law, or the prophets; I am not come to destroy, but to fulfill" (Matt. 5:17). He looked at His cross and said, "The Son of man goeth as it is written of Him" (Matt. 26:24). He told Peter that He didn't need the protection of his sword, for if He wished He could call down thousands of angels for assistance. "But how then, shall the Scriptures be fulfilled, that thus it must be?" (Matt. 26:54). Jesus came to fulfill Scripture. His view of Scripture was that it was all about Him and every detail had to be fulfilled.

In a strong statement concerning Scripture, Jesus said, "Scripture cannot be broken." He meant that what God said was true and what was prophesied would take place. He even compared the duration of Scripture to the duration of the universe. He said, "It is easier for heaven and earth to pass, than one tittle of the Law to fail" (Luke 16:17). "All things that are written by the prophets . . . shall be accomplished" (Luke 18:31).

Jesus' view of Scripture then was that it was the Word of God and that what was written was certain to come to pass. He even called attention to the individual words.

The psalmist predicted that when the Messiah died on the cross, He would cry out, "My God, My God, why hast Thou forsaken Me?" (22:1) While dying on the cross, Jesus cried out, "My God, My God, why hast Thou forsaken Me?" (Matt. 27:46) Psalm 22 also foretold that the suffering Saviour would thirst. On the cross Jesus cried out, "I thirst" (John 19:28).

Jesus believed in every word of the Old Testament. He corroborated the great truths of the Old Testament. For example,

He confirmed the creation of Adam and Eve, in effect stating that what the Old Testament says about them is true. He said, "Have ye not read, that He which made them at the beginning made them male and female, and said, 'For this cause shall a man leave father and mother, and shall cleave to his wife; and they twain shall be one flesh'?" (Matt. 19:4-5) Jesus believed in the real Creation as recorded in Genesis.

Jesus and the Record

Some have attempted to allegorize the murder of Abel. But Jesus, in a confrontation with the Pharisees, said, "From the blood of Abel unto the blood of Zacharias, which perished between the altar and the temple; Verily I say unto you, It shall be required of this generation" (Luke 11:51). Here Jesus made reference to the slaying of Abel as an actual event.

Throughout the years people have also denied the historical nature of the Flood. They don't like to recognize that human sin made the Flood a necessity. But Jesus believed in the Flood. He declared, "But as the days of Noah were, so shall also the coming of the Son of man be. For as in the days that were before the flood they were eating and drinking, marrying and giving in marriage, until the day that Noah entered into the ark" (Matt. 24:37-38).

He substantiated many other facts in the Book of Genesis—such as the destruction of Sodom and Gomorrah and the turning of Lot's wife into a pillar of salt. In Mark 12 we read that He affirmed the call of Moses, and in John 6 He talked about the manna from heaven. He referred to the brazen serpent lifted up in the wilderness by which Israel was healed (John 3). Over and over again, Jesus confirmed the authority of the Old Testament record.

Jesus also established the sufficiency of the Scripture to save men. In the account of the rich man and Lazarus, the Lord quoted Abraham from the perspective of Paradise, saying,

"They have Moses and the Prophets; let them hear them" (Luke 16:29). He was saying that the brothers of Lazarus didn't need one to rise from the dead in order for them to be saved. The testimony of the prophets was sufficient to bring them to the knowledge of the truth.

Jesus also spoke of the ability of Scriptures to keep one from error, referring to those who erred because they didn't know the Scriptures (Mark 12:24, 27).

There is an interesting statistic about the Lord's use of Old Testament Scriptures. Of the 1,800 verses in the New Testament which include quotations of Jesus, 180 of them, or one-tenth, come from the Old Testament. He who is the truth, He who is the Word, believed and submitted to the inspired writings of the Old Testament without reservation. If He was committed to that, I'm certainly willing to be. If Jesus believed in the Old Testament Scriptures, I believe them also.

In looking at the testimony of Jesus about the Scriptures, we have to accept one of three possibilities: There are no errors in the Old Testament, as Jesus taught; there are errors, but Jesus didn't know about them; there are errors that Jesus knew about, but He covered them up.

If the second is true—that the Old Testament contains errors of which Jesus was unaware—then it follows that Jesus obviously wasn't God and we can dismiss the whole thing. If the third alternative is true—that Jesus knew about the errors but covered them up—then Jesus wasn't honest, or holy.

I accept the first proposition: The Scripture is indeed the revelation of God, inspired to give us an infallible record of God's dealing with men. Belief in the deity of Jesus Christ demands a belief in the verbal plenary inspiration of Scripture.

The Final Witness
We have considered the witness of the Bible writers and the witness of Jesus. We must also call the Holy Spirit as a wit-

ness. The belief that the Bible is the inspired Word of God is not the result of an intellectual decision. Rather it is the result of the work of the Holy Spirit in a person's life. An individual won't believe the Bible until the Holy Spirit has done His work of convincing him.

Let's sketch the argument. We believe the Bible is true because the Bible says it is true. "That's circular reasoning," someone objects. Good point. If a person doesn't believe the Bible, he is not going to believe the Bible when the Bible says that it is the Word of God. On the other hand, if a person accepts the Bible as the Word of God, it is because the work of the Holy Spirit caused that truth to dawn on him.

People are not so stupid that they can't understand the truth; they are hostile because they don't want to accept the truth. People do not want to include God in their knowledge, so when they hear the preaching of the Cross they consider it foolishness (1 Cor. 1:21). The natural (unregenerate) man doesn't receive the things of God (1 Cor. 2:14). In order for his abnormal, depraved mind to receive the truth of God, the Holy Spirit must work.

It is, therefore, impossible by argument, or by preaching alone, to cause someone to believe the Bible. Everyone is dependent on the internal work of the Spirit, but the Spirit cannot produce belief in the Word of God until a person has heard the Word of God. Paul asked, "How then shall they call on Him in whom they have not believed? And how shall they believe in Him of whom they have not heard? And how shall they hear without a preacher?" (Rom. 10:14)

Time for Decision

Our case is finished. We have looked at the testimonies of the Old Testament writers and of the New Testament writers, of the Lord Jesus Christ and of the Holy Spirit—all defending the inspiration of the Bible. It is a solid case. The only possible verdict is that the Scriptures are indeed God's inspired Word.

What should be our response to this fact? We must practice Colossians 3:16: "Let the Word of Christ dwell in you richly." Our minds should be a tablet where the Word of God is written. We are to read it, obey it, and apply all of its teachings in our lives. Finally, we are to pass it on.

It has been estimated that in one lifetime the average citizen will consume 150 head of cattle, 2,400 chickens, 225 lambs, 26 sheep, 310 pigs, 26 acres of grain, and 50 acres of fruits and vegetables. That's a lot of food.

How much of the Word of God are we consuming? An outdoor bulletin board at a church in Quincy, Massachusetts carried this message. *A Bible that is falling apart usually belongs to someone who isn't.*

We have in the Bible a genuine treasure.

5
Difficulties in the Bible

Until recently the great controversy concerning the Scriptures was most frequently fought between skeptics outside the church and Christians. Now skeptics inside the church espouse the heresy that the Bible contains errors. What is taught in the Bible, they say, may or may not be true. The Bible can't be trusted in every part.

This is an extremely serious charge because the integrity of Jesus Christ rests on the doctrine of the verbal plenary inspiration of the Bible—that the Bible is the Word of God. We can't have a divine Saviour and an errant Bible, because Jesus said it was without error. We can't have an infallible Bible and no Saviour, because all of Scripture testifies of Christ.

There are three general areas in which the critics attack the Bible. First, they say the Bible is not inspired because it disclaims inspiration—that in some passages the Scripture denies that it is inspired.

For example, the Apostle Paul distinguishes between his instruction concerning marriage and the Lord's instruction (1 Cor. 7). At first glance, Paul seems to be saying that perhaps some of his writings are not inspired. "But I speak this by permission, and not of commandment" (v. 6). Paul was saying that he was permitting something but not commanding it. He was okaying an action, but not ordering it. That something is being married. Paul wrote, "Let every man have his own wife, and let every woman have her own husband" (v. 2). If he had stopped there, we would be in trouble because all the single people in the church would be living in disobedience. He goes on to say marriage isn't something that one has to do.

In fact, Paul even backs off a little way from this position. "I would that all men were even as I myself. But every man hath his proper gift of God, one after this manner, and another after that. I say therefore to the unmarried and widows, It is good for them if they abide even as I" (1 Cor. 7:7-8).

Not everyone has the gift of remaining single, therefore Paul adds, "If they cannot contain, let them marry: for it is better to marry than to burn" (v. 9). People may disagree about what *burn* means, but I think the correct interpretation is *to burn with passion*.

Paul, then, is saying that every man may have his own wife, and every woman may have her own husband, but he is not commanding marriage, because some may have the gift of singleness. His statement is not in any way a disclaimer to inspiration.

Paul's Personal Opinion?

To say that Paul's writing is somehow on a lesser level of inspiration opens the door to all kinds of antibiblical practices. For example, some groups disregard Paul's teaching that women are not to usurp authority in the church and that women are not to serve as elders (1 Tim. 2:12; 3:2). We see major denominations torn by dissension over whether women should be ordained, preach, and administer the ordinances.

They don't accept what Paul wrote because they think he

was giving his personal opinion about the role of women in the church, and that Paul was old-fashioned and antifeminist in his viewpoint.

The critics raise questions about 1 Corinthians 7:10 and 12. "And unto the married I command, yet not I, but the Lord, Let not the wife depart from her husband" (v. 10).

Paul was saying, "I am telling you something that didn't originate with me. It originated with the Lord. I am quoting Jesus." He goes right back to the Lord's words:

It hath been said, whosoever shall put away his wife, let him give her a writing of divorcement: But I say unto you that whosoever shall put away his wife, saving for the cause of fornication, causes her to commit adultery: and whosoever shall marry her that is divorced commits adultery (Matt. 5:31-32).

In other words, Jesus said, "Stay together!" Paul is echoing those words. He is saying, in effect, "Now when I say to you to stay married, it's not just I saying it; it's the Lord who commanded it."

Paul continues. "But to the rest speak I, not the Lord: If any brother hath a wife that believeth not, and she be pleased to dwell with him, let him not put her away" (1 Cor. 7:12). Paul is saying that he is no longer quoting Jesus. This does not mean that what he writes is not inspired. Paul does not minimize his own teaching; it is also inspired. He only distinguishes it from the words of Jesus.

I once met a man who believed only the red letter portions of the New Testament—those which are the words of Jesus. I don't like red-letter Bibles because they imply that what Jesus said is more inspired and authoritative than what Paul said. That isn't true. In the case in point, Paul was giving additional revelation to what the Lord had said.

When Paul wrote "I say to you," he was not minimizing his words. Remember that as we go through the Bible we have progressive revelation which means that God revealed further truth through the apostles (John 16:12).

Copying the Original

In another area of criticism, the Bible is said to be full of errors because of the process of transmission over a long period of time. These critics may acknowledge that the original auto-graphs of the Bible were without error, but they say we don't have any original autographs remaining today. "How do you know what you have is the same as the original?" they ask. They point to the fact that parts of the Bible were written thousands of years ago, and that down through the centuries, as it was copied and recopied, mistakes have crept in.

What is the answer to this criticism? Certainly the original manuscripts have been copied. This work was done by scribes, or copiers. These were specially trained and dedicated men who took on the copying process. They followed principles of checking and rechecking. Their work was long and painful and demanded extreme care. Because they believed that they were copying the Word of God, they were extraordinarily precise. It is said that Ezra the scribe could recite the entire Old Testament word perfect.

Christian scholars have taken up the study of Bible manuscripts with as great an intensity. It is exciting to realize that in the opinion of most scholars today, the Bible text that we hold in our hands is practically identical to the original. Is that any surprise? If God inspired the writing of the Bible, He can certainly take care of its transmission.

Do you realize that the Bible, though it is an ancient Book, has been established with greater certainty than any other ancient book in existence? Thousands of Bible portions preserved on scrolls and parchments have been discovered in Bible lands. And the more that are discovered, the more we see they agree in content. A manuscript of one part is found in one place, and another manuscript of the same text is found in another place. Put them side by side and they are alike. From two different cultures, from two different periods of time, from two different scribes, the manuscripts are the same. The fact that researchers come up with manuscripts that say the same thing is a powerful argument for the purity of the text.

Textual scholars have noted some human errata occasioned by a scribe copying a wrong letter or vowel pointing, or inverting a word order, but these errors amount to less than one word in every thousand. In fact, only one out of every 1,580 words in the Old Testament has any kind of variation from other manuscript copies.

Consider the famous Dead Sea Scrolls. You may recall the story of how, in 1947, a shepherd boy was trying to chase a sheep out of a cave. He threw a rock inside and heard a piece of pottery break. He went in and discovered vessels holding ancient scrolls. These were portions of the Old Testament. A manuscript of Isaiah was among them.

Until 1947 Bible scholars had been basing their translations on the Masoretic text (ca. AD 800–1000). With the unveiling of the Dead Sea Scrolls, they had a text going back before the time of Christ! On making comparisons, they found that the Masoretic text was essentially the same as the Dead Sea text copied hundreds of years earlier. There were no substantial differences.

The Lord Jesus said that Scripture cannot be broken (John 10:35). The manuscripts of the Old Testament to which Christ referred were those in the people's hands at the time. Most likely they were equivalent to the Dead Sea Scrolls. That is important because when Jesus said that the Word of God was without error, He was referring to Scripture of the same generation as the Dead Sea Scrolls. He was establishing the authority of those manuscripts. There is no reason to doubt that our present Old Testament, based on the Masoretic text and the Dead Sea Scrolls used several centuries before Christ, is anything but reliable and essentially what God authored in the original autographs.

When someone comes along and says we have transmission problems in the Bible, we can deny it. The same God who put it together originally has preserved it. If God can prepare the original writers to set down His Word without error, He can safeguard the copiers. Jesus said, "My words shall not pass away" (Matt. 24:35).

There is a third area in which critics attack the Bible. They contend that there are errors in the Bible that cannot be reconciled.

There are no errors in the Bible, but there are difficulties. Parts of the Scripture are difficult to harmonize; however, such difficulties disprove collusion on the part of writers. If the Bible were a fraud, it would agree with itself on every last point.

Some difficulties are the result of misunderstanding the culture in which the Bible was written. Sometimes we don't understand the geography or the history of the time, or we have difficulty trying to figure out the meaning of Hebrew or Greek words used thousands of years ago.

Difficulties in the Bible indicate that God's ways are higher than our ways. We can well sympathize with Peter. He wrote of Paul's letters that he found "some things hard to be understood" (2 Peter 3:16). "That Paul—he's hard to understand!" Peter makes us smile, but we know exactly what he meant.

Nevertheless, let's consider several of the difficulties that critics raise and see if we can discover answers. An old question is, Where did Cain get his wife? The answer is easy—he married his sister.

"But that's forbidden," you say.

Yes, but the prohibition came along many centuries after

the time of Cain. If there was only one family to start, it is obvious that there had to be intermarriage in that first family. In Genesis 5:4-5, we read that Adam begat many sons and daughters over his lifetime of 930 years. And Adam's sons and daughters became parents of other sons and daughters. Cain could have chosen his wife from many women.

All That Glitters

Critics used to attack the 18th chapter of 2 Kings, which recounts the struggle between Sennacherib, king of Assyria, and Hezekiah, king of Judah. When Sennacherib attacked, Hezekiah sought peace and said, "'I have done wrong. Withdraw from me; whatever you impose on me I will bear.' So the king of Assyria required of Hezekiah, King of Judah 300 talents of silver and 30 talents of gold" (v. 14, NASB).

Archeologists digging around in modern times found some interesting information about this transaction—data that apparently contradicted the Bible. They discovered that Sennacherib's official account called for 800 talents of silver and 30 talents of gold—quite a discrepancy.

Critics concluded that the Bible is in error. They rejected the thought that Sennacherib could make a mistake, and they failed to take into consideration that they were dealing with later manuscripts rather than with the original record.

Archeologists continued to dig in their search for more information about this famous ancient empire. More recent discoveries brought to light the fact that while the standard for calculating gold was the same in Assyria as in Judah, the standard for figuring silver was different. They learned, in fact, that 800 Assyrian talents of silver were equal to 300 Jewish talents. So again, the Scriptures proved to be right, even to the very numbers. Only further insights and additional information were needed.

What about the area of theology? Critics like to say that Paul and James disagree. First they point out that Romans 4:1-4 declares that Abraham got his salvation by faith, not by works. Then they compare that with James 2:21: "Was not Abraham our father justified by works, when he had offered Isaac his son upon the altar?"

"This is an absolute contradiction," the critics maintain. "One teaches justification by grace and faith, and the other justification by works."

If we study these passages carefully, we find something very interesting. Paul is referring to Abraham in Genesis 15, while James is referring to Abraham in Genesis 22. Paul goes back to the time when Abraham was first redeemed and declared righteous. In Genesis 15 Abraham believed God and was saved by faith. But James goes back to the time when Abraham offered Isaac as a visible indication of the reality of his faith. One is saying that a man is saved by faith; the other is saying that true salvation becomes visible through good works. There is no disagreement, no contradiction at all. Once again we see that careful study on a scholarly level often melts away apparent difficulties. The Bible stands despite all of these assaults.

On the Attack

That is defense. What about offense? One positive is the uniqueness of the Bible. No book like it exists. If we don't believe God wrote it, then we have a problem. Doctor Montiero Williams, a professor of Sanskrit, spent 40 years studying Eastern books, and said:

> Pile them, if you will, on the left side of your study table, but place your own Holy Bible on the right side, all by itself and with a wide gap between them, for there is a gulf between it and the so-called sacred books of the East that severs the one from the other utterly, hopelessly, and forever (Sidney Collett, *All About the Bible*, Revell, pp. 314–315).

Take, for example, the sacred writings of the Hindus and you find such fantastic nonsense as this:

The moon is 50,000 leagues higher than the sun and shines by its own light. Night is caused by the sun setting behind a huge mountain several thousand feet high and located in the center of the earth. This world is flat and triangular and is composed of seven stages: one of honey, another of sugar, a third of butter, and another of wine, and the whole mass is born on the heads of countless elephants which in shaking produce earthquakes.

Read the Koran and you find that the stars are nothing but torches in the lower heavens, and that men are made out of baked clay. The grossest kinds of errors abound in Greek and Roman mythology, in the wild and disordered books of the Hindus, and in the traditions of the Buddhists and the Moslems. There is not one such absurdity in the Bible!

One of a Kind

The Bible is *unique*. It has been read by more people, published in more languages, studied, and criticized more than any other book. God wants it circulated, and it is being circulated. The Bible was the first major book to come off of the Gutenberg press in 1456. By 1932 the London Bible Society said there were one and one-half billion Bibles in print. Nobody knows how many billion there are now.

The Bible is the only Book that gives the account of special Creation. It is the only Book that gives a continuous historical record from the first man to the present era and on into the future. It is the purest religious literature with the highest moral standards. It is the only Book of antiquity containing detailed prophecies of events to come. It is the only Book that convicts people of sin and leads them to salvation. There is no book in the world like the Bible.

We know the Bible is true as evidenced by its uniqueness,

but it is also characterized by *unity*. Such unity comes from one author guiding the whole. There are 66 books from 40 or more human writers, ranging over 1,600 years beginning with Moses who wrote the first book of the Bible, to the Apostle John who wrote the last book.

One wrote in Syria, another in Arabia, another in Italy, still another in Greece. Others wrote in the desert of Sinai, the wilderness of Judea, the cave of Adullam, the prison in Rome, the barren island of Patmos, in the palaces of Zion and Shushan, along the rivers of Babylon, and in other places. The Bible was written in several languages, reflected different lifestyles and occupations, describes different events in a variety of locations. The Bible contains poetry, history, theology, proverbs, parables, allegories, and more; yet it is one harmonious whole: a mastermind inspired it and preserved it.

Lay out the pattern of the Bible and you find four themes—revelation, history, devotion, and prophecy. In the Old Testament the first five books, the Pentateuch, constitute revelation. Then comes history, Joshua to Esther. Then comes devotion, Job to the Song of Solomon. Then comes prophecy, Isaiah to Malachi. In the New Testament, the Gospels give history; the Book of Acts, devotion; the Epistles, prophecy; and the final book gives revelation.

Consider just the theme of salvation in the Bible. In the Gospels we have salvation effected; in the Acts, salvation preached; in the Epistles, salvation explained; in the Revelation, salvation fulfilled for perfect continuity.

I think the Bible vindicates itself by its *indestructibility*. Because the Bible is God's Word, it partakes of God's nature. Since God is eternal, so is the Bible. "Forever, O Lord, Thy Word is settled in heaven" (Ps. 119:89).

Throughout history Satan has used many means and men to attack the Bible. Diocletian, the Roman emperor, mounted the most concerted attack ever against the Bible. He killed so many Christians and burned so many manuscripts that he finally erected a column and called it *Extincto Nomine Christianorum,* which means, "The name of Christians has been extinguished." He was mistaken. Soon the Roman Empire adopted Christianity as its official religion.

The Word Goes On

Pseudoscience has tried to laugh the Bible out of existence. A century ago, Voltaire, the famous French writer and atheist, declared, "Fifty years from now the world will hear no more of the Bible." But in that very year, while a first edition of Voltaire's book was selling for 8¢ a copy, the British Museum was paying the Russian government $500,000 for one New Testament Greek manuscript copy. And 50 years after his death, the Geneva Bible Society used Voltaire's house and press to print Bibles.

Thomas Paine wrote *The Age of Reason* 200 years ago, and in it he attacked Christianity. He felt his arguments would forever destroy the Bible. He predicted that in a few years the Bible would be out of print. He boasted, "When I get through, there will not be five Bibles left in America." He turned out to be a little off in his count.

It has been said that unbelievers with all their attacks on the Bible make no more impression than a man would with a toy hammer on the pyramids of Egypt.

So the hammers of infidels have been pecking away at this book for ages, but the hammers are worn out and the anvil still endures. Praise God for His Word. United. Unique. Indestructible.

"The grass withers, and the flower falls, but the Word of the Lord abides for ever" (1 Peter 1:24-25, RSV).

6
Miracles in the Bible

For some people, miracles in the Bible constitute a big problem. If we could get rid of the miracles more people would believe the Bible, they say.

On the other hand, I believe that the Bible is truly the Word of God and the fact of miracles is a good demonstration of that fact. In ordinary conversation we use the term *miracle* loosely. We say, for example, "I was driving home last night and you'll never believe what happened. A guy went right through a red light and barely missed me. I'm telling you; it was a miracle!" Or, "I didn't have any money and unexpectedly I got a check for $50 in the mail. I praise God for this miracle!" We make everything miraculous.

But what precisely is a miracle? Webster's Dictionary gives a poor definition, but one that fits the modern mentality. It says a miracle is "an event or effect in the physical world deviating from the known laws of nature, or transcending our knowledge of these laws." Notice that this does not say that a miracle deviates from the laws of nature but rather from the *known* laws of nature. Webster explains miracles then as a natural phenomena, not supernatural ones.

Webster's definition does not apply to the miracles of the Bible. The implication Webster leaves is that a miracle is a happening that can't be explained. In the Bible a miracle can be explained as an event that happens because God intervenes in the workings of the natural world and does something supernatural.

By way of illustration, think of our world as a little box. Everything in our box is qualified by natural law. God occasionally pokes His finger into our box and "makes waves." God intervenes.

In the New Testament, miracles are described in three terms: signs, wonders, and mighty works. Miracles are mighty works to create wonders to act as signs. Signs are not ends in themselves—they point to something. Miracles are not ends in themselves, they point to Someone.

Two Options

There are two responses to the signs of miracles. One is the atheist's reaction. He says naturalism is all there is; God does not exist. Miracles are impossible since there is no supernatural. This is what some unbelievers maintain, but as a result they have difficulty explaining where the universe came from in the first place.

The other response is that of the Christian. He accepts the fact that there is a spiritual, supernatural power. He believes in God. For him, miracles are believable because the supernatural is there to act upon the natural. In fact, if there is a God, miracles are to be *expected*. Otherwise we would be merely affirming that God is and not expecting Him to do anything. If God is, then God acts because being necessitates doing. If God is, miracles are valid.

Anybody who believes in God *must* believe in miracles. We can't approach the Bible and say, "I'll accept this as the Word

of God provided I can ignore the miracles recorded in it."
That is the same as saying, "Okay, God. You can exist, but
You can't do anything that reveals Yourself." In order for a
miracle to fit the biblical definition, it must have three quali-
ties. First, it must be verifiable—perceived by the senses. It
must be something that we can see or hear or feel and give
testimony to.

Second, a miracle must be clearly miraculous. It must tran-
scend all natural law. There is no other explanation than it is a
revelation of the power and presence of God.

And third, there must be a divine purpose to the miracle.
God performs miracles to reveal to us His person. Miracles,
then, must be perceived by the senses; they must be clear, and
they must have a divine purpose.

As we read through the Bible, we find that miracles in the
Word of God fit all of these qualifications. The miracles recorded in Scripture were seen or experienced by credible witnesses. They are clearly beyond natural explanation, and they
have a divine purpose of pointing people toward God. While
we can't examine all the Bible miracles because of space limita-
tions, we can consider some of each kind: miracles that affected all people, miracles that affected nations, and miracles
that affected individuals.

Universal Miracles

The first miracle is found in the first verse of the Bible: "In
the beginning God created the heaven and the earth" (Gen.
1:1). The Bible starts out with the assumption that God is.
There is no argument in the Scriptures for the existence of
God. It is not a theory to be proven; it is a fact to be affirmed.
The Bible never attempts to prove that God exists.

If a person declares that there is no God, the burden of
proof rests on him. When an atheist says, "I don't believe
there is a God," I reply that I believe there is a God because

the Bible affirms there is a God. He must prove to me that there is not a God, and of course, he can't do it.

If we accept the first sentence of the Bible, we have no problem with the miracle involved. The word *created* means "to make out of nothing." If we believe God made everything out of nothing, we believe in a miracle. And if we believe the miracle of Genesis 1:1, why should we doubt the other miracles recorded in the Bible?

The miracle of Creation is certainly the greatest one in terms of scope. Can you imagine how God stepped out on the edge of nothing and made everything—by His Word alone? That is a miracle!

As we look at Genesis 1, we stand in amazement at how simply the Spirit of God describes this: "And the earth was without form, and void; and darkness was upon the face of the deep. And the Spirit of God moved upon the face of the waters" (v. 2). God created and the creation was formless. Then the creation takes form: "Let there be a firmament in the midst of the waters, and let it divide the waters from the waters. And God made the firmament, and divided the waters which were under the firmament from the waters which were above the firmament: and it was so" (vv. 6-7).

In the remainder of Genesis 1 we have a detailed and beautiful description of the Creation. Some people say, "This is just a myth. This isn't how it really happened."

Yet the description in Genesis 1 contains no scientific errors. Not one statement has ever been conclusively proven wrong. Even the sequence of the Creation matches with what scientists have discovered. For example, if you check botany sources, you will discover that the order in which the flora and the fauna are said by the Genesis account to have appeared on the earth corresponds with that which the theory of evolution requires and the evidence of geology proves.

Moses was no geologist, and he certainly wasn't around during the Creation to observe firsthand, but what Moses wrote is true because God revealed it to him.

How Long a Time?

Scientists stumble over the Bible statement that all of the Creation took place in six days. They reject this because they hold to the geological age system. They say that billions of years ago the elements and the stars and the galaxies evolved, without explaining what they evolved from. They might say that five billion years ago the earth and the solar system evolved. Three billion years ago the evolution of life took place. Fifty million years ago the ancestors of apes and men evolved. Three million years ago modern man evolved.

Scientists frequently base their calculations on the fossil record. They find fossils in sedimentary rock, so they determine that the fossils are a certain age because they are found in that rock. Then they reverse that reasoning by saying that a rock is a certain age because of the fossils it contains.

Some propound a view called theistic evolution or progressive creationism. "We believe the Genesis account," they insist, "only those weren't actual days. Those verses refer to great blocks of time—millions of years." They insist that they must allow for great time periods for the strata of the earth to be formed as we now observe them.

But is all that time really required? The distance from my work to my home may be five miles. If I want to get to my home, I could crawl. That would take me a very long time. Or I could walk all the way home in less time. Or I could get in my car and "drive like a jehu." I would cover the same ground, only at different speeds.

God didn't need a lot of time for forming things if He ran the Creation at a high speed. And that may be how God did it.

If you took a leaf and laid it on a brick, it would never become a fossil by such a slow process. But if a catastrophe suddenly occurred and slammed that leaf into a rock and hermetically sealed it, then you would have a fossil. And that is a better explanation of how the fossils in the sedimentary rock got there.

If you allow for a period of time being speeded up, there is no problem. It is possible to take a 33⅓ record and play it at 78 rpm. It may sound like Alvin and the Chipmunks, but it will cover exactly the same content.

I believe the Bible when it says that God created the world in six days. I think God knows how to communicate. He has a vocabulary that is accurate.

The Hebrew word for "day" used in Genesis is *yom*. When in the plural it means a literal day. In six days the Creation took place. God didn't need time and a slow pace.

The miracle of Creation, then, is clear. It is sensible. How can you verify the miracle of Creation? Look up. Look around you. It is obvious that One with awesome power is the Creator and Sustainer of the universe. It is verifiable. It proves God to me. Only God could do it. It is absurd to think that everything came from nothing.

How Did He Do It?

Consider a second miracle as recorded in Genesis 6 and 7—the Flood. God told Noah to build an ark 450 feet long by 75 feet wide by 43 feet high out in the middle of a desert! "And the Lord said unto Noah, Come thou and all thy house into the ark; for thee have I seen righteous before Me in this generation" (Gen. 7:1). Then God went on to give specific details about the animals that were to enter the ark.

"The whole thing is ridiculous," some people might say. "How was Noah to determine which animals should go and which must stay behind and be drowned?"

It was no problem for the God who made those animals. God has much less trouble with animals than He does with people: "The ox knows his owner, and the ass his master's crib: but Israel does not know, My people do not consider" (Isa. 1:3). God organized the animals to do His will.

When the animals went into the ark, God broke up everything: "All the fountains of the great deep [were] broken up, and the windows of heaven were opened. And the rain was upon the earth 40 days and 40 nights" (Gen. 7:11-12). Water covered the entire earth. Mount Ararat was about 17,000 feet high, and water covered that mountain. Since water seeks its own level, that indicates a universal flood.

In the Creation and in the Flood we have two great events that have given us our present world. Men explain the natural effects with theories that call for long passages of time, but Scripture states that through catastrophic means God speeded up the processes so that the Creation, which took six days, shaped the earth, and the Flood, which lasted approximately 150 days, reshaped it.

Another miracle, recorded in Genesis 11, concerns the Tower of Babel. Men set out to build a ziggurat, a pagan tower, to worship a false god. So the Lord did an interesting thing:

And the Lord said, Behold, the people is one, and they have all one language; and this they begin to do. And now nothing will be restrained from them, which they have imagined to do. Come let us go down, and there confound their language, that they may not understand one another's speech. So the Lord scattered them abroad from thence upon the face of all the earth: and they left off to build the city. Therefore is the name of it called Babel (Gen. 11:6-9).

The word *babel* comes from the Hebrew word meaning "to confuse." So the Lord confused the language of all the earth and scattered the people. Here is a very clear and responsible explanation of where languages came from. God performed a miracle that affected all mankind.

Creation revealed God as Creator. The Flood revealed God as Saviour. Babel revealed God as Judge. All of them fulfilled the divine purpose of pointing to God.

National Miracles

Now let us look at a second category of miracles—those that have affected nations. A good example concerns the Children of Israel at the Red Sea, an account given to us in Exodus 14.

We can imagine the situation in which Moses and the Israelites found themselves. They were camped between two mountains. Behind them came Pharaoh and the Egyptians with all their horses and chariots. Before them lay the Red Sea. We can understand why they would cry out to the Lord (v. 10).

"And the Lord said unto Moses, Wherefore criest thou unto Me? Speak unto the Children of Israel, that they go forward" (v. 15). "Okay, Lord," Moses must have said, "but how are we going to do it?"

But lift thou up thy rod, and stretch out thine hand over the sea, and divide it: and the Children of Israel shall go on dry ground through the midst of the sea. And I, behold, I will harden the hearts of the Egyptians, and they shall follow them: and I will get Me honor upon Pharaoh, and upon all his host, upon his chariots, and upon his horsemen. And the Egyptians shall know that I am the Lord (vv. 16-18).

Here again God is revealing Himself. He is performing a miracle to show that He is God. Would there be any doubt about that back in the capital of Egypt when they discovered that their entire army had been drowned?

And the angel of God, which went before the camp of Israel, removed and went behind them; and the pillar of the cloud went from before their face, and stood behind them. And it came between the camp of the Egyptians and the camp of Israel; and it was a cloud and darkness to them, but it gave light by night to these: so that the one came not near the other all the night (vv. 19-20).

God placed his Shekinah Glory between the Egyptians and the Israelites to disturb the one and to comfort the other. And Moses stretched out his hand over the sea; and the Lord caused the sea to go back by a strong east wind all that night, and made the sea dry land, and the waters were divided. And the Children of Israel went into the midst of the sea upon the dry ground; and the waters were a wall unto them on their right hand, and on their left. And the Egyptians pursued, and went in after them to the midst of the sea, even all Pharaoh's horses, his chariots, and his horsemen. . . . And the Lord said unto Moses, Stretch out thine hand over the sea, that the waters may come again upon the Egyptians, upon their chariots, and upon their horsemen. And Moses stretched forth his hand over the sea, and the sea returned to his strength when the morning appeared; and the Egyptians fled against it; and the Lord overthrew the Egyptians in the midst of the sea. And the waters returned, and covered the chariots, and the horsemen, and all the host of Pharaoh that came into the sea after them; there remained not so much as one of them (vv. 21-28).

How Did It Happen?

It was a miracle. There is no other logical explanation for it, though some have been offered. Some critics have said that at the north end of the Red Sea was an area called the Bitter Lakes or the Reed Sea. Between the Red Sea and the Bitter Lakes was a little marshy area where the water was only two or three inches deep. According to the proponents of this theory, a southeast wind blew up the channel and the stiffness of the wind held the water in the Bitter Lakes and the tide ebbed away in the Red Sea. This, they say, enabled the Israelites to wade through the marshy area.

That is weak—really weak. To the best of our knowledge, the Bitter Lakes and the Red Sea were fairly well separated. And even if the Israelites did march through one, two, or three inches of marshy area, how were all the hosts of the Egyptians drowned in that place? It takes more faith to believe that explanation than it does to believe the biblical account.

What did account for the strong east wind that parted the waters? The breath of God. God walled up the waters on both sides by a miracle. If we believe in God, then we should believe in this miracle. How stupid for a puny little man to stand up and say, "No, God, You couldn't have done it that way. You must not act supernaturally."

In Exodus 16 we read about the miracle of the manna (vv. 14-22). God provided His people with manna to eat during the 40 years of their wandering in the desert. Skeptics have suggested some amazing explanations of this provision. Some explain manna as lichen, which grows on rocks and trees. The lichen was increasing in volume day after day, they say, and the people collected this and ate it as their food. But researchers believe there was no such thing in the desert of Sinai, at least there has been no trace of it in the last several hundred years.

Another suggestion is that the manna was really a sticky, light-colored, honeydew excretion that came out of tamarisk twigs. The people went along scraping this substance from the tamarisk bark.

But investigators have discovered that the substance on the tamarisk isn't produced by the tamarisk at all, but is left there by insects. And besides, the substance only appears during the months of June and July, and it would hardly have been sufficient to feed 3 million people.

The provision of manna was a miracle. God fed His people

with something that He created especially for them. And if God is God, He could do that easily enough.

In addition to miracles that have affected all people and miracles that have affected nations, the Bible contains miracles that have affected individuals. Consider the fascinating account recorded in Numbers 22 concerning Balaam. Balaam was a prophet for hire, and he was doing the wrong thing.

And God's anger was kindled because he went, and the angel of the Lord stood in the way for an adversary against him. Now he was riding on his ass, and his two servants were with him. And the ass saw the angel of the Lord standing in the way, and his sword drawn in his hand; and the ass turned aside out of the way, and went into the field: and Balaam smote the ass, to turn her into the way (vv. 22-23).

Balaam became angry and struck his animal. He didn't see a thing, but the ass saw the angel of the Lord with a big sword. Balaam probably rode the donkey every day. But now all of a sudden the animal had gone crazy, wandering all over, and injuring the rider. No wonder Balaam was angry.

What follows is very interesting: "And the Lord opened the mouth of the ass, and she said unto Balaam, What have I done unto thee, that thou hast smitten me these three times?" (v. 28)

You say, "Nobody would ever believe that. No sane individual would ever believe that Balaam's ass talked!" But I can refer you to one who did—one of the most sane individuals in all the Bible, one of the most precious saints of God who ever lived. The Apostle Peter had this to say about the false teachers of his day: "Which have forsaken the right way, and are gone astray, following the way of Balaam, the son of Beor, who loved the wages of unrighteousness; but was rebuked for his iniquity; the dumb ass speaking with man's voice forbade the madness of the prophet" (2 Peter 2:15-16). Peter believed this miracle, and Peter was a credible witness.

Let us return to the account in Numbers 22: "Balaam said unto the ass, Because thou hast mocked me: I would there were a sword in mine hand, for now would I kill thee" (v. 29). The miracle is not that the ass spoke to Balaam—it is that Balaam answered! I think I would have fallen flat on the ground in astonishment.

Suggested Answers

What about the person who wants to believe in God but who can't believe that this miracle took place? One said that Balaam was in a trance and mistakenly thought he heard the animal speak. Another critic has suggested that Balaam had a habit of talking to himself. He was merely replying to himself, and the witness mistook it for the talking of an animal. Yet another has said that Balaam was so used to talking to his donkey that when the donkey talked back to him, Balaam was just misinterpreting the familiar bray. They just won't admit to the possibility of a miracle.

This incident is certainly a miracle, and what astounds me is the writer's total lack of defensiveness in relating it. If I were writing this down, I would say, "Folks, I'm about to say something that you're not going to believe. There was this guy riding on his donkey, and. . . ." I would have to preface the story with a few little statements to prepare the readers for the jolt.

Here is something amazing about Bible writers: No matter how strange or unbelievable the miracles may seem, the writers never defend them. They only state and affirm.

Who recorded this account of Balaam and his ass? Moses, the man who was elevated to the highest place in Pharaoh's court, the man who, with his genius of leadership, led at least 3 million people in the wilderness. Moses was the man to whom God communicated the Ten Commandments and other aspects of the Law. He was the man who wrote the Pentateuch with its deep truths and great doctrines, the man who wrote the sweeping history of the beginning. This man, without self-consciousness and without one defensive statement, wrote about the conversation between Balaam and his donkey.

In this and other miracles recorded in the Bible, I see a God of action—one who intervened in the world in supernatural ways. I find this exciting. These accounts enlarge my concept of an all-powerful God and increase my desire to know Him better.

7

The Miraculous Jesus

We have defined a miracle as an act of God by which He temporarily sets aside natural law and does something supernaturally. God's miracles are always purposeful. He doesn't act in an irrational, nonsensical, haphazard way. In contrast, the happenings related in the apocryphal books are irrational. One of these so-called miracles, for example, says that when Jesus was a little child He would take clay and make pigeons. Then He would tap them and they would suddenly come to life and fly away. It is also recorded in one source that Jesus got mad at the other children and killed them.

Such accounts violate the character of Jesus Christ as we know it from Scripture. They also violate the teaching of Scripture itself. When Jesus turned water into wine, the Scripture says, "This *beginning* of miracles did Jesus in Cana of Galilee" (John 2:11, author's italics). That was His first miracle.

Miracles were never done merely to entertain people. They were done purposefully to reveal God and what He is like. They showed Him to be loving and kind and merciful, but also to be just. Old Testament miracles disclosed the nature of God. Those performed by Jesus and recorded in the Gospels verified the deity of Christ. They certified that Jesus was none other than God Himself. We read in the Gospel of John, "Therefore the Jews sought the more to kill Him, because He not only had broken the Sabbath, but said also that God was His Father, making Himself equal with God" (5:18). They abhorred His statement that "all men should honor the Son, even as they honor the Father" (John 5:23).

What proof is offered that Jesus is on the same level as God? We get a clue from John 5:31 and 32: "If I bear witness of Myself, My witness is not true. There is another that beareth witness of Me; and I know that the witness which he witnesseth of Me is true." Here Jesus is referring to the testimony of John the Baptist.

There is still a further witness. "But I have greater witness than that of John; for the works which the Father hath given Me to finish, the same works that I do, bear witness of Me, that the Father hath sent Me" (v. 36).

The greater testimony to the Lord's deity is His works. If a person comes along and says, "I am God," we disregard it for lack of proof. We believe that Jesus was God because He not only claimed to be, but He supported the claim by His works. In John 10 this idea comes across clearly: "Then came the Jews round about Him, and said unto Him, 'How long dost Thou make us to doubt? If Thou be the Christ, tell us plainly.' Jesus answered them, 'I told you, and ye believed not; the works that I do in My Father's name, they bear witness of Me'" (vv. 24-25).

New Testament Miracles

Verification that Jesus is the living Word of God is largely based on the miracles that He performed. As Christians we don't have to apologize or stand ashamed at the record of miracles. Miracles give validity to the claim that the Bible is the Word of God and to Christ's claim that He was the Son of God.

I find miracles convincing. John the Baptist did. When he was in prison, John sent two of his disciples to Jesus to ask Him, "Art Thou He that should come? Or look we for another?" (Luke 7:19) In contemporary language we would ask, "John wants to know if you are the Messiah that he's been announcing?"

Jesus didn't launch into a long answer. Instead, "In that same hour He cured many of their infirmities and plagues, and of evil spirits; and unto many that were blind he gave sight" (v. 21). Jesus proved that He was the Messiah by performing miracles. "Then Jesus answering said unto them, 'Go your way, and tell John what things ye have seen and heard; how that the blind see, the lame walk, the lepers are cleansed, the deaf hear, the dead are raised, to the poor the Gospel is preached'" (v. 22). They probably rushed to report to John what they had seen.

Convincing arguments for the deity of Christ are seen in His works as well as in His words. The Bible is seen as the Word of God because it contains miracles, and that means God is in the Book. And Jesus is God because He performed miracles.

In the Bible, we have an exciting record of a unique personality. Historian Philip Schaff wrote in his book *The Person of Christ:*

This Jesus of Nazareth without money and arms conquered more millions than Alexander, Caesar, Mohammed, and Napoleon. Without science and learning He has shed more light on things human and divine than all the philosophers and scholars combined. Without the eloquence of schools He spoke such words of life as were never spoken before or since and produced effects which lie beyond the reach of orator or poet. Without writing a single line, He has set more pens in motion and furnished themes for more sermons, orations, discussions, learned volumes, works of art, and songs of praise than the whole army of great men of ancient and modern times (Josh McDowell, *Evidence That Demands a Verdict,* Campus Crusade for Christ, p. 26).

Schaff was a believer, but even the skeptic H. G. Wells testified, "When I was asked which single individual has left the most permanent impression on the world, the manner of the question almost carried the implication that it was Jesus of Nazareth. I agree" (*Reader's Digest,* May, 1935).

The Miracle of Jesus' Birth

Everything about Jesus was miraculous. First, His birth was miraculous. The opening book of the New Testament contains the credible, responsible testimony of a man named Matthew: "Now the birth of Jesus Christ was on this wise: When as His mother Mary was espoused to Joseph, before they came together, she was found with child of the Holy Ghost" (Matt. 1:18). She was pregnant—but not by Joseph.

"Then Joseph her husband, being a just man, and not willing to make her a public example, was minded to put her away privily" (v. 19). He had two choices: He could bring her out into the middle of the street to be stoned to death for the sin of adultery, or he could divorce her with as little fuss as possible.

Joseph assumed that a terrible tragedy had happened— Mary had had sexual relations with another man, even though Joseph and she were pledged as spouses. His heart must have been heavy.

But while he thought on these things, behold the angel of the Lord appeared unto him in a dream, saying, "Joseph, thou son of David, fear not to take unto thee Mary thy wife: for that which is conceived in her is of the Holy Ghost. And she shall bring forth a son, and thou shalt call his name *JESUS:* for He shall save His people from their sins." Now all this was done, that it might be fulfilled which was spoken of the Lord by the prophet, saying, Behold, a virgin shall be with child, and shall bring forth a Son, and they shall call His name Emmanuel, which being interpreted is, God with us (vv. 20-23).

Who was Jesus then? "God with us." What a marvelous promise and fulfillment of messianic prophecies that go back to Genesis 3:15 which foretold the coming of One who would be unusually born. God said, "I will put enmity between thee and the woman, and between thy seed and her seed." But what woman ever had seed? That is the function of the man. Only once in history did woman have a seed, and that woman was Mary. The Spirit of God created it within her. What a marvelous birth! It was special creation. God didn't need a man to impregnate Mary. God instantly created an embryo.

"Oh," you say, "that's biologically impossible!"

Of course it is. That is why we know God did it. It was also biologically impossible to create Adam out of dirt, but God did it. And it was biologically impossible to create Eve out of the side of Adam. But God did that too. Biological impossibilities are no problem for God. He is supernatural.

All the historical evidence agrees that the early church believed from the beginning in the virgin birth. Some people say, "Oh, they just made it up." That can't be true because the Jews never believed their Messiah would be born this way, so why would they invent something they never anticipated?

Other people say, "The Jewish Christians invented the virgin birth." But they never anticipated it, either. They were shocked. Why did the early church believe this doctrine—because they made it up? No, because it was true.

Let the skeptics and the doubters rail against the miraculous birth of Christ, if they will. They can't undo it. They can't shake it. God set aside the normal requirements of two human parents in order to bring forth His only Son, born of a virgin. He was the God-Man.

The Miracle of a Sinless Life

This direct creative act of God bypassed the sin problem. Whatever is born of the flesh is flesh. Jesus was not born of the flesh, but of the will of God. And that led to the miracle of our Lord's sinless life.

That Jesus did not begin to exist at the time of His birth is implied in His words, "For I came down from heaven, not to do Mine own will, but the will of Him that sent Me" (John 6:38). And the opening words of John's Gospel declare plainly, "In the beginning was the Word, and the Word was with God, and the Word was God. The same was in the beginning with God" (1:1-2). The Lord has always existed. There never was a time when He was not.

Did John the Baptist know that? Check his testimony: "This was He of whom I spoke, He that cometh after me is preferred before me: for He was before me" (1:15).

The theme of the Lord's preexistence is carried out repeatedly on the pages of this Gospel. Jesus told the Pharisees, "'Your father Abraham rejoiced to see My day: and he saw it and was glad.' Then said the Jews unto Him, 'Thou art not yet 50 years old, and hast Thou seen Abraham?' Jesus said unto them, 'Verily, verily, I say unto you, Before Abraham was, I am'" (John 8:56-58). Jesus could do something with grammar that no one else can do. He could say, "I am yesterday; I am today; I am tomorrow." Only the eternal God could make such a statement.

What a life He lived! Hebrews 4:15 makes the amazing statement, "For we have not an high priest which cannot be touched with the feeling of our infirmities; but was in all points tempted like as we are, yet without sin." Think of that: *Jesus never sinned!*

"For such an high priest became us, who is holy, harmless, undefiled, separate from sinners, and made higher than the heavens" (Heb. 7:26). That too speaks of His sinless life.

Even Judas with his twisted and sick mind recognized that Jesus was sinless. He said, "I have sinned in that I have betrayed the innocent blood" (Matt. 27:4). This unbeliever confessed that Jesus had never sinned.

Other unbelievers made the same judgment. Pilate said five times, "I find no fault in Him" (Luke 23:4, 14; John 18:38; 19:4, 6). The thief on the cross said, "We indeed [suffer] justly; for we receive the due reward of our deeds: but this Man hath done nothing amiss" (Luke 23:41, author's brackets). And the Roman centurion saw that Jesus was faultless (Matt. 27:54).

It is useless to look through the entire biography of Jesus hoping to find a single stain or the slightest shadow on His moral character. Jesus never had to cry out as David did, "Create in me a clean heart, O God" (Ps. 51:10). Nor recount the battle between the old and new, as Paul did (Rom. 7). Jesus could never have died, as Saint Augustine did, reciting penitential psalms. Jesus needed no forgiveness. He needed no grace. He had no sin. Jesus lived a miraculous, sinless life, the result of His supernatural birth.

Supernatural Words

A third area of the miraculous in the life of Jesus is His unsurpassed words. Sholem Ash was quoted by Frank S. Mead in *The Encyclopedia of Religious Quotations* as having said:

Jesus Christ is the outstanding personality of all time. . . . [The teaching of] no other teacher—Jewish, Christian, Buddhist, Mohammedan—is such a guidepost for the world we live in. Other teachers may have something basic for an Oriental, an Arab, or an Occidental, but every act and word of Jesus has value for all of us. He became the Light of the world. Why shouldn't I, a Jew, be proud of that? (Revell, p. 49)

You can't read through the New Testament and not be impressed with the words of Jesus. They are startling! The Pharisees dispatched the temple police to arrest Jesus, but they came back empty-handed, their eyes wide, and reported, "Never man spoke like this man" (John 7:46).

Like His birth and His sinless life, the words of Jesus were miraculous. He taught about God, angels, men, earth, heaven, hell, past, present, and future. He posed questions no man could answer, and He answered questions that were unanswerable by others. Nicodemus came to Him in the night and said, "We know that Thou art a Teacher come from God" (John 3:2). How did he know it? By what Jesus had to say. His words were supernatural.

Add His Works

Jesus' supernatural works were another area of the miraculous. Even as Nicodemus was impressed by the words of Jesus, so he was impressed by His works: "No man can do these miracles that Thou doest, except God be with Him" (John 3:2). Nicodemus was not at this time a believer or a follower of Jesus. He was a teacher of the highest rank in Israel. Yet it was obvious to him that God was in Christ because of what He was able to do.

The record of history shows that Jesus performed miracles on a nonselective basis. He healed all kinds of people with all kinds of diseases. There were no situations He could not handle, and the miracles of Jesus were never temporary.

There are several categories into which the miracles of our Lord fall. The first shows His power over nature. He commanded nature, and nature obeyed. For example, He turned water into wine.

Weddings were big affairs in those days. The celebration lasted an entire week. To serve wine was a practical necessity. To run out of wine was a social offense, but it happened at a wedding in Cana. Jesus told the servants to fill the huge 20- or 30-gallon water pots with water, and when they had done so, He ordered, "Take some out to the steward." The steward tasted the water that had been miraculously turned into wine and said, "This is unusual! Ordinarily at the end of the wedding the wine is inferior, when people no longer are as sensitive to the taste, but this wine is the best I've ever tasted at a wedding."

Isn't it interesting that apparently no fanfare was associated with this first miracle of Christ? There is no record that the angels sang or heaven shook or the earth rattled. Jesus did not climb on the roof and shout out over the assembly, "Wine!"

I think Jesus probably just looked at those stone water pots and that was it. For the One who created the universe, a few gallons of wine was a small thing. There were plenty of witnesses who corroborated this miracle. And John recorded it in his Gospel (2:1-11).

On another day Jesus stood on the side of a hill at the Sea of Galilee. There probably were 20,000 people gathered around him—5,000 men plus women and children. From the loaves and fishes of one little boy's lunch, Jesus fed them all. On that occasion alone, all of those people witnessed the power of Jesus Christ (John 6:1-14).

He stilled a storm (Mark 4:39). He looked at the waves pounding around Him and said, in effect, "It's time for you to cease." And they did. He walked on water (Matt. 14:25). When it came time to pay His taxes, He directed Peter to a fish with the money inside its mouth (Matt. 17:27). Disappointed at finding no fruit on a fig tree, He ordered that no fruit grow on it and that it wither (Matt. 21:18-22). In these and other ways He commanded nature, and nature obeyed.

The Great Physician

Jesus also showed His power by healing disease (second category of His miracles). He healed a leper (Luke 5:12-15). He healed a paralytic (Mark 2:1-12). He healed Peter's mother-in-law (Mark 1:29-31). He healed the nobleman's son (John 4:46-54). He healed a withered hand (Mark 3:1-5). He healed the deaf and dumb (Mark 7:31-37). He healed blindness (John 9:1-34). He healed 10 lepers (Luke 17:11-19). And a short time before He was nailed to the cross, He healed the ear of Malchus that Peter had cut off (Luke 22:49-51).

A third category of the miracles of our Lord concern His power over the grave. He confronted death, and death yielded up its prey. There was the daughter of Jairus (Mark 5:22-43) and the son of the widow (Luke 7:11-15). But the one I love best is the story of Lazarus (John 11:1-46). Jesus came to the grave and ordered the stone rolled away. Martha protested. She thought Jesus merely wanted to pay His respects and to say good-bye. She didn't understand what was about to happen.

Prayer. Silence. Then a shout: "Lazarus, come out!" And Lazarus came out. The people were so shocked that Jesus had to tell them what to do—to unwrap the grave clothes. I don't know who removed the cloth from Lazarus' face, but I don't think I could have done it. I would have been immobilized by shock.

Reactions—Ancient and Modern

Julian the Apostate, a Roman emperor from 361 to 363, had a vehemently anti-Christian reaction to Jesus. Philip Schaff quotes him as having said, "Jesus . . . has now been celebrated about 300 years, having done nothing in His lifetime worthy of fame, unless anyone thinks it a very great work to heal lame people and blind people and exorcise demoniacs in the villages of Bethsaida and Bethany" (*The Person of Christ*).

Julian could not have been more wrong.

This leads us into another area of the miraculous in Jesus' life—His power of influence. Consider that the destiny of every person in the world depends on the Lord Jesus Christ. There is no salvation apart from Him (Acts 4:12). Paul declared that "at the name of Jesus every knee should bow, of things in heaven, of things in earth, and things under the earth; and that every tongue should confess that Jesus Christ is Lord, to the glory of God the Father" (Phil. 2:10-11).

Ernest Renan, the French atheist, said, "Jesus is in every respect unique, and nothing can be compared with Him." Napoleon said, "I know men, and I tell you Jesus Christ is no mere man. Between Him and every other man in the world there is no possible term of comparison."

Jesus' impact on people is unequaled in the history of humanity. Two thousand years later the impact is not diminished in any way. Every day people have life-changing experiences as they consider His claims and enter into a personal relationship with Him. Is it not astounding that this very day anyone can turn his life over to this historical Person who lived 2,000 years ago and know an instant and eternal transformation? Jesus is without parallel or equal.

I find this exciting. Some people may think of Jesus as ancient history, but to Christians He is alive—He is the living Christ. He is the master of hungry crowds and angry Pharisees, clever theologians and bitter sinners, stupid disciples, and smart governors—Jesus is master of them all.

He is master of Himself. He struggled in the olive groves in the midnight hours before His death. He fought sweat, blood, and tears, and came forth victorious, completely dedicated to God and His will.

In the terrible agony of the Cross, He was Master. Fury was all around Him, but He was calm and in control. He passed forgiveness on to a penitent thief and opened the door of Paradise to him. He remembered His mother and His beloved John. When the effects of the loss of blood, shock, trauma, exposure, and the torture of crucifixion got to Him, He calmly fulfilled the last prophecy by saying, "I thirst" (John 19:28). Then, in obedience to the Father's will, He died.

No one has been conceived as Christ was. No one has lived as He lived. No one has died as He died. No one compares with Him. He has influenced the world.

Jesus made some amazing statements and promises:

I am the way, the truth and the life; no man comes unto the Father, but by Me (John 14:6). The Son of man has power upon earth to forgive sins (Matt. 9:6). Whosoever therefore shall confess Me before men, him will I confess also before My Father which is in heaven (Matt. 10:32). No man knows the Son, but the Father; neither knows any man the Father, save the Son, and he to whomsoever the Son shall reveal him (Matt. 11:27). I am the resurrection, and the life: he that believes in Me, though he were dead, yet shall he live: And whosoever lives and believes in Me shall never die (John 11:25-26). Whosoever will lose his life for My sake . . . shall save it (Mark 8:35). I am the Light of the world; he that follows Me shall not walk in darkness, but shall have the light of life (John 8:12). Whosoever drinks of the water that I shall give him shall never thirst (John 4:14). Come unto Me, all ye that labor and are heavy laden, and I will give you rest (Matt. 11:28). Heaven and earth shall pass away, but My words shall not pass away (Luke 21:33). Before Abraham was, I am (John 8:58). On this rock I will build My church; and the gates of hell shall not prevail against it (Matt. 16:18). I am the door of the sheep. All that ever came before Me are thieves and robbers (John 10:7-8). I and My Father are one (John 10:30). I am the bread of life: he that comes to Me shall never hunger (John 6:35).

Victory over Death

Jesus raised others from the dead, but we also see His miraculous working in His own resurrection. From the cross He watched as prophecy was fulfilled. Then He said, "I thirst," and He died. He was buried, and when the time came for Him to leave the grave, He left. The tomb was empty, and it has been empty since the day He left it. There is abundant Scripture and historical evidence to support the resurrection of Christ. Should that be surprising? Death is a natural consequence, but God is supernatural. Christ not only conquered death for Himself, but for us as well. Because He lives, we shall live also (John 14:19).

As we look at the life and miracles of Jesus, we can only conclude that He was God. And if we accept that proposition, all else logically follows. If God became man, we would expect Him to have a unique and miraculous entrance into this world. Jesus did.

If God became man, we would expect Him to be sinless and to live a godly life. Jesus did.

If God became man, we would anticipate His words to be clear, authoritative, true, and pure. Jesus' words were all of these. "Never man spoke like this Man" (John 7:46).

If God became man, we would expect Him to manifest supernatural power. Jesus did that.

If God became man, we would expect Him to have a universal and permanent influence on the lives of men. Jesus does.

If God became man, we would expect Him to exercise power over death. Jesus did.

God *did* become man. His name was Jesus of Nazareth—Jesus the Christ, worker of miracles.

8
Science
and
the
Bible

Many have taken on themselves the task of making discrediting statements about the Bible and science. Aldous Huxley said, "Modern science makes it impossible to believe in a personal God." Philosopher Bertrand Russell said:

Man is the product of causes which had no pre-vision of the end they were achieving. His origin, his growth, his hopes, his fears, his loves and beliefs are but the outcome of accidental collocation of atoms. . . . All the labors of the ages are destined to extinction in the vast death of the solar system.

It seems that as science advances and verifies more data and more technology, there is a movement on the part of some scientists to eliminate the necessity of God. Once God was almighty; now science is almighty. Scientists who hold to a position called *scientism* say that as they find explanations of natural phenomena, God becomes smaller and smaller.

Christians are constantly being confronted with a supposed conflict between science and Scripture. We are told that Christianity doesn't gain the respect of a scientific world because it makes nonscientific statements and blunders. Men say that we have to choose science or religion, that we can't have both. Either the "facts of science" or the "fantasy of Scripture"—we must decide which.

And so the clash goes on, based on the fact that both science and the Scripture claim total authority. Let me suggest that there is no real conflict between science and Scripture—none. A great difference exists between science and scientism. Scientism constitutes the theories of a scientist who is wearing glasses with philosophically tinted lenses.

There is no real conflict between the Bible and science. We can be Christians and at the same time very capable scientists. Throughout history, for example, such outstanding men as Galileo, Kepler, Descartes, von Leibnitz, Newton, and Pascal were respected both as Christians and as scientists.

What's in a Word?

It is true that the Bible doesn't use scientific jargon, but that doesn't make the Bible nonscientific. Suppose you are enjoying a Thanksgiving Day turkey, and someone asks, "Would you like more?" In scientific language you might reply, "Gastronomical satiety admonishes me that I have arrived at a state of deglutition consistent with dietetic integrity." Which means, "No thanks, I've had enough!"

We don't expect the Bible to be written in scientific jargon. It is written in everyday language so everyone can understand it. We do not disparage the Word of God and say it is nonscientific because it doesn't use current scientific language. For example, when the Bible says "the sun stood still," it is from man's view—just as we say "sunrise" and "sunset" though scientifically it is "earth revolving."

Once we get over that hurdle of terminology, there is no real conflict between science and Scripture. The conflict comes when science stops being science and starts being religion. Science, by its very definition, can deal only with that which is observable, that which is reproducible. Whenever it goes beyond reproducible, and starts talking about origins and destinies, it becomes religion. It is jumping to things that cannot be observed. That is where the conflict lies.

Yet many Christians assume that the Bible is full of scientific error. The whole movement known as liberalism has already bowed to this concept. Its proponents agree that the Bible is full of scientific error, so they have given up on it. Their typical statement runs this way: "The Bible is only authoritative when it speaks on spiritual matters. When it speaks on scientific matters, we have to handle it allegorically and spiritually, because it is prone to error." They are saying that the God who wrote the Bible knew a lot about the spiritual, but not about science.

To say that the parts of the Bible dealing with the spiritual may be true, but the parts about science are false is ridiculous for two reasons. First, such a stance denies the inspiration of God in the Scripture. If God is God, then He knows as much about science as He does about the spiritual.

Also, such a position denies the inerrancy of Scripture, that the Bible has been properly recorded. If God is the author, it is inspired and inerrant and just as right scientifically as it is spiritually. God can only speak truth. "Thy Word is truth" (John 17:17). The New Testament declares that God cannot lie (Titus 1:2). There is nothing that He does not know. He is omniscient. When science sets itself against God's revelation, it ceases to be science. It becomes ignorance. It becomes a religion of ignorance.

The scientist who practices scientism isn't content to observe what is going on *now*. He extrapolates into the past and into the future and discusses origins and destinies. But that isn't science. He can't put the past into a test tube because the past isn't reproducible. Science can only observe the present—that is all. It can only deal with the observable activity in a microscope, telescope, or test tube.

While it is true that the scientist has some past history of tests and experiments to lean on, he inevitably wants to go back into prehistorical time. When he goes back to before his history was recorded, he is talking about what is nonobservable. It is not reproducible. It cannot be made scientific; therefore, his speculations about prehistoric origins become, of necessity, a matter of faith.

As an example of how science works, consider the theory called uniformity, which says that everything going on at the present rate has always gone on at the same rate and will always continue to go on at the same rate.

The scientist going through his experiment of natural processes today, says it takes such and such a time to do this and to do that. Then he goes back and extrapolates his uniformity concept. Holding to the idea that everything in the past proceeded at the same rate it does in the present, he concludes that man is millions of years old, and that the earth is billions of years old.

Does he really know that? No, because he has no information about the prehistoric past. Very little was written before the Old Testament period, even though people were people. They were not hanging in trees by their tails and they were not in the process of becoming human as evolutionists would have us believe.

It is impossible for us to prove scientifically that the scientist is wrong at this point. A Christian can't say, "You've struck out, fellows. I'm going to show you your error." That can't be done because the events of that time are not reproducible. They are not subject to scientific checking. Evolution can't be reproduced, but neither can Creation. We must turn to divine revelation from the God who has been there through it all.

Another View?

"Well," you may ask, "what does the Bible teach about this matter?" The Bible teaches that in six days God made everything. I believe it teaches that God acted in great catastrophies. The theory of catastrophe is set against the theory of uniformity as an explanation of what might have happened or what is going to happen. Two books that deal with the subject of catastrophe are *The Genesis Flood* by John Whitcomb and Henry Morris, and *Many Infallible Proofs* by Henry Morris.

The Bible also teaches that in the future Jesus is going to return and create a new heaven and a new earth. The Scripture's view on this comes through Peter. He wrote:

There shall come in the Last Days scoffers, walking after their own lusts, and saying, "Where is the promise of His coming? For since the fathers fell asleep, all things continue as they were from the beginning of the creation." For this they willingly are ignorant of, that by the Word of God the heavens were of old, and the earth standing out of the water and in the water, whereby the world that then was, being overflowed with water, perished. But the heavens and the earth, which are now, by the same Word are kept in store, reserved unto fire against the day of judgment and perdition of ungodly men (2 Peter 3:3-7).

Peter is pointing out that those people who think that all things are going to continue as they were in the past and are at present have forgotten that history shows this is not true. Examples are the Flood in the days of Noah and the Day of Judgment to come. The theory of uniformity doesn't hold water, if I may be allowed a pun. I believe we see the theory of catastrophism laid out for us in the Creation and in the Flood. It boils down to this: Either we believe in uniformity that can't be proven, or we believe in catastrophism for which I think there is support in the Bible.

With that in mind, I repeat that there is no conflict between science and the Bible. There is only conflict on a moral basis between men and God. Because ungodly men don't like to retain God in their knowledge (Rom. 1:28), they hold to their doctrine of uniformity. That, I say, takes greater faith than to believe in the Bible.

A good illustration is found in a newsletter in which one scientist candidly admits, "I reject the idea of a transcendent God, so what other option do I have?" This shows that his decision is a moral one, not a scientific one.

The issue is not between science and Scripture. The issue is whether or not a man wants to submit to the Word of God. Most have rejected God, and they have to come up with some explanation. They reject revelation for imagination. If God didn't create, they reason, the universe "just happened."

How Science Works

Scientists generally hold to several basic principles: Science must deal with *things* (matter), with *happenings* (energy), and with a matrix in which those things happen (*space-time*). So the basics of science are matter, energy, and space-time. The universe must be a continuum of matter, energy, space, and time. One of these cannot exist without the other. All must work together. This continuum must have existed from the beginning of life.

This is exactly what we read. "In the beginning God created the heaven and the earth." That includes matter, energy, and the space-time matrix. The first verse of the Bible tells us that God created the three basic dimensions of science simultaneously from the beginning of life.

Once the universe had been created in its processes, scientists say, it was designed to operate in an orderly fashion. All the different phenomena were ordered and sustained by these forces. Science says that the forces continue and continue and continue. No further creation was needed.

The Bible says this too: "God ended His work which He had made" (Gen. 2:2). When He had put it all together, He stopped and the Creation ended right there. Matter is never totally lost. Time and space continue.

The complete cessation of creative activity has been recognized by modern science as the first law of thermodynamics. It is the law of the conservation of mass and energy—one of the most universal and most certain of all scientific principles. Science has shown that there is nothing being created in the known universe at this time. Changes are occurring that affect matter and energy, but nothing is being created. The Bible says that when God ended His work, He ended it! That fits the scientific facts.

Written in the Word

The Bible, of course, supports the first law of thermodynamics. "Lift up your eyes on high, and behold who has created these things, that brings out their host by number. He calls them all by names by the greatness of His might, for that He is strong in power. Not one fails" (Isa. 40:26). Here is the law of the conservation of mass and energy.

Scientists "discovered" what they called the first law of thermodynamics. They really discovered the truth of Isaiah 40:26.

Read also Nehemiah 9:6: "Thou, even Thou, art Lord alone; Thou hast made heaven, the heaven of heavens, with all their host, the earth, and all things that are therein, the seas, and all that is therein, *and Thou preservest them all*" (author's italics).

Even Solomon recognized this. "The thing that hath been, it is that which shall be; and that which is done is that which shall be done; and there is no new thing under the sun" (Ecc. 1:9). Here is yet another clear statement about the continuation of creation: "Is there anything whereof it may be said, 'See, this is new'? It hath been already of old time, which was before us" (v. 10).

Science says the totality of mass and energy occurred because of evolution. Believers say that God made it, but notice that at least they both agree on the truth of the conservation of matter and energy. In Ecclesiastes 3:14-15 we read, "I know that, whatsoever God does, it shall be forever: nothing can be put to it, nor anything taken from it. . . . That which hath been is now, and that which is to be hath already been." Isn't that amazing? The Word of God is absolutely accurate in defending and defining the first law of thermodynamics, the conservation of mass and energy.

Law Number Two

There is a second law of thermodynamics: the law of increasing disorder. It says that though there is never a loss of mass and energy, its ability to produce breaks down and down and down. Order becomes disorder. All processes will finally cease and the universe will be dead, scientists tell us.

"Does that fit Scripture?" you ask.

It certainly does. But God didn't make the world with the second law of thermodynamics operating. God made the world and He looked at it and said, "It is good." Only when man sinned did the second law of thermodynamics come into being.

Science has never been able to figure out how that law works or where it came from. But we know it came from the Fall of man. After man fell, God said, "Cursed is the ground" (Gen. 3:17). That was simply the symbol of the curse that reached everywhere.

Look at Romans 8 for insights on the second law of thermodynamics.

For the creature [creation] was made subject to vanity,

not willingly, but by reason of Him who hath subjected the same in hope, Because the creature itself also shall be delivered from the bondage of corruption into the glorious liberty of the children of God. For we know that the whole creation groans and travails in pain together until now (vv. 20-22).

The curse that came on man and his world explains for me the second law of thermodynamics.

At present we have disorder, a breaking down, an entropy existing in nature, but this condition is only temporary (Rom. 8:20-22). Why? Because the Lord will come and create a new heaven and a new earth. There will be no second law of thermodynamics operating in the kingdom of God in its final form. The Bible promises no more curse, no more death, no more tears, no more sorrow, no more crying, no more pain, no more regrets, no more exile, no more trouble, no more hurting, no more destruction, no more decay, no more unrighteousness, no more night, no more sin!

The Water Cycle

Hydrology is basically the science that deals with the cycles followed by the waters of the earth. Water from the ocean is evaporated up in the atmosphere and collected in the clouds. It is redeposited on the earth as rain or snow. Water from this rain and snow runs into streams, then rivers, and eventually winds up in the ocean. Water evaporates from the ocean, and the cycle continues. Some of the rain and snow that falls seeps into the ground and provides water for our use.

This whole cycle of hydrology puzzled the world until the 17th century. Before that, people had believed in subterranean reservoirs, which were supposed to exist deep in the middle of the earth. They thought the springs came from those reservoirs.

Then the concept of hydrology was introduced. Science had

at last discovered and defined the evaporation, transportation, and precipitation aspects of the water cycle.

If people had only read Isaiah 55, they would have had the problem solved for them: "For as the rain and the snow come down from heaven, and do not return there without watering the earth, and making it bear and sprout, and furnishing seed to the sower and bread to the eater" (v. 10, NASB). There is the cycle. God deposits the rain; it saturates the earth, is recollected, evaporated, brought up from the seas and from the dry land and cycled back to the clouds again. That is scientifically accurate. We also read that the Word of God has this same cycle effect, for God used the hydrology information to illustrate the effectiveness of His Word: "So shall My word be that goes forth out of My mouth, it shall not return unto Me void, but it shall accomplish that which I please, and it shall prosper in the thing whereto I sent it" (v. 11).

Ecclesiastes 1:6-7 provides more information: "The wind goes toward the south, and turns about unto the north; it whirls about continually, and the wind returns again according to its circuits. All the rivers run into the sea; yet the sea is not full; unto the place from whence the rivers come, thither they return again." Do you know why the sea doesn't become full, even though all the rivers keep running into it? Because it is the same water. It just keeps cycling. Solomon pointed that out a long time before the 17th century.

We read more on the subject in the Book of Job. "For He maketh small the drops of water; they pour down rain according to the vapour thereof, which the clouds do drop and distill on man abundantly" (36:27-28). The oldest book in the Bible describes the process of evaporation and precipitation.

We also read that God "causes the vapors to ascend from the ends of the earth; He makes lightnings for the rain; He brings the wind out of His treasuries." So the Scripture gives the hydrological cycle and the features of evaporation.

In Job we can also learn about condensation (26:8), and about the runoff of water (28:10). The psalmist wrote about the ocean reservoirs (Ps. 33:7). And God asked Job, "Hast thou entered into the treasures of the snow? Or hast thou seen the treasures of the hail?" (Job 38:22) Clouds store snow and hail. The Bible contains facts that men have begun to understand only recently. God made the whole hydrological cycle, and told us about it in His Word.

Look Up
In the field of astronomy we also see agreement between the Bible and science. New ideas on the solar system didn't begin to replace the old ones until the 17th century. The prevalent theory had been that the earth was round and flat. People thought that if one were to sail through the Pillars of Hercules, which is the Rock of Gibralter, he would fall off into nothingness.

When Copernicus (1473–1543) came along and presented his theory that the earth was in motion, people thought he was out of his mind. Then came men such as Brahe, Kepler, and Galileo in the 17th century, and they gave birth to modern astronomy which tells us of the infinite size and variety of the universe. They conceived of the universe as staggering in size.

Were they the first to learn that? The Prophet Isaiah wrote about how high the heavens were above the earth. He was quoting the Lord (55:9). In Job, the oldest book in the Bible, we read, "Is not God in the height of heaven? And behold the height of the stars, how high they are!" (Job 22:12). Jeremiah referred to the solar system as vast and distant: "Thus saith the Lord, If heaven above can be measured, and the foundations of the earth searched out beneath, I will also cast off all the seed of Israel for all that they have done, saith the Lord" (Jer. 31:37).

Before the telescope was invented in the 17th century,

Hippartus said there were 1,022 stars. But Ptolemy said, You missed it. The number is 1,056. Then Kepler said, You're both wrong, fellows. There are exactly 1,055. Jeremiah testified, "The host of heaven cannot be counted" (33:22, NASB). Today scientists tell us there are more than 100 billion stars in our galaxy alone. How many billion galaxies there are, only God knows! There is no more a way of counting the stars than there is of counting the grains of sand on the shores of this earth.

Science has recently discovered that each of the stars is different. Yet the Bible has been saying that all along: "There is one glory of the sun, and another glory of the moon, and another glory of the stars; for one star differs from another star in glory" (1 Cor. 15:41). Now if the Bible had said, "All the stars are the same," then you could set the Bible aside as wrong. But the Word of God is not wrong—on this or on any other point. It is reliable. God knows as much about stars as He does about salvation.

Written in the Rocks

Geology, the science of the earth, is another area where there is no contradiction between science and the Bible. Consider the field called isostasy—the study of the balance of the earth. This wasn't fully understood until about 1959. The earth has been found to be perfectly balanced with an equal weight to support land mass, mountains, valleys, and water. The equilibrium of all this is nothing less than astounding.

For example, the ocean exerts a pressure against the shore that keeps the mountains up. Rock masses have different weights at different places to balance it out. Though this is a fairly recent discovery, look at what Isaiah wrote long ago: "Who has measured the waters in the hollow of His hand, and meted out heaven with the span, and comprehended the dust of the earth in a measure, and weighed the mountains in scales, and the hills in a balance?" (Isa. 40:12) Who else but God?

"He [God] established the earth on its foundations, so that it will not totter forever and ever" (Ps. 104:5, NASB, author's brackets). "The mountains rose; the valleys sank down to the place which Thou didst establish for them" (v. 8). God made the earth so that it balanced.

Again and again there is no contradiction between science and the Bible. The same God who wrote the Bible is the God who made the world and the universe.

The concept of a spherical earth (Isa. 40:22) helps us to interpret an interesting passage in the New Testament. Referring to the Second Coming, or just prior to it, Luke wrote:

> In that day, he which shall be on the housetop, and his stuff in the house, let him not come down to take it away: and he that is in the field, let him likewise not return back. Remember Lot's wife. Whosoever shall seek to save his life shall lose it; and whosoever shall lose his life shall preserve it. I tell you, in that night there shall be two men in one bed; the one shall be taken, and the other shall be left (Luke 17:31-34, NASB).

If you look at this passage carefully, you will notice that the word *day* is used (v. 31) and then the word *night* (v. 34). How can it be both day and night when the Lord returns? Because of the existence of a spherical earth. That explains how some can be working and some sleeping. Anybody who thought that the earth was flat didn't understand the significance of this Scripture.

In the 17th century Isaac Newton added to our understanding of the earth when he defined the law of gravity. But thousands of years before, Job had said, "He hangeth the earth on nothing" (26:7). So the Bible teaches a suspended spherical earth.

The Bible is accurate not only in such areas as hydrology,

astronomy, and geology but also in meteorology. The basic principle of meteorology is the circulation of the atmosphere. In the 17th century Galileo discovered that wind travels in circuitous patterns. Galileo was behind Solomon, who lived about 900 B.C. Solomon said, "The wind goes toward the south, and turns about unto the north; it whirls about continually, and the wind returns again according to his circuits" (Ecc. 1:6).

Before Galileo, no scientist had determined that air had weight. But Job said long before that, "He [God] imparted weight to the wind" (28:25, NASB, author's brackets). Again, the Bible is accurate in its scientific information.

A Look at the Body
The Bible also is accurate in the science of physiology. In 1628 William Harvey discovered that the circulatory system is the key to life. Only then was it understood that circulation of the blood is critical in keeping a person alive. Before that, whenever someone was sick, the doctor removed blood through a bleeding process. But now doctors give blood to the sick. This agrees with the Book of Leviticus where we read, "The life of the flesh is in the blood" (17:11).

"That verse is referring to a spiritual truth," you may say. Yes, it does refer to the ancient sacrificial system, but it is correct as it relates to physical life as well. The Bible doesn't make mistakes. Essentially, in many of the illustrations I have given, it is spiritual truth that is the issue, but when Scripture touches on a scientific theme, it is just as inerrant as in the spiritual theme.

In 1953 a medical book entitled *Personality Manifestations and Psychosomatic Illness* came out. It pointed out that emotions can cause debilitating and even fatal illnesses. The book diagramed the emotional center of the brain from which nerve fibers descend to every area of the body. The diagram demonstrated how trauma, any emotional stress or turmoil in the center, can send out impulses through the fibers of the nerve system and cause anything from headaches to foot itch and even more serious ailments.

According to the book, the emotional center produces illness in three ways. First, it changes the amount of blood flow. For example, when a person is angry, the blood rushes to his face. Emotional stress, then, can increase or decrease the amount of blood flow.

Second, emotional stress at the center of the nervous system can affect secretions of certain glands. Have you ever been very nervous before you were to give a speech—so much so that your mouth dried up? Your brain sent certain impulses through your nervous system that dried up the glands that provide fluid in your mouth. Excess thyroxin (an iodine) is produced by emotion. When too much thyroxin is poured into the bloodstream, it can produce goiter and even fatal heart disease.

Third, emotions can change physical health by creating muscle tension. The nerves affect the muscles and the muscles tighten up and become tense.

The Word of God anticipated what science has so recently discovered about the relationship of emotions to physical health. "Pleasant words are as an honeycomb, sweet to the soul, and health to the bones" (Prov. 16:24). God knew that emotional stress—anger, criticism, and sour words—can affect physical health. God revealed it: "A merry heart does good like a medicine: but a broken spirit dries the bones" (Prov. 17:22). A happy person is a healthy person. An unhappy person is an unhealthy person. Psalm 32 tells us that David's anxiety over sin dried up his life juices (vv. 3-4). We have touched lightly on the areas of hydrology, astronomy, geology, meteorology, and physiology. And if space permitted we could delve into biology, archaeology, anthropology, and all the other "ologies." We would find that each time the Bible speaks on these areas, it is absolutely accurate. What scientists have only recently discovered was declared in the Bible long ago.

How can this be? There is only one answer. God is the author of this Book and the revealer of the truth it contains.

Instead of refuting Scripture, science properly understood, confirms it. To pit science against the Bible is foolish and unnecessary. I am convinced that in the final analysis all truth—scientific and spiritual—is one. As Jesus said, "Thy Word is truth" (John 17:17). The Bible speaks the truth at all points because God inspired its writing.

9
Writing History before It Happens

One of the great indications of the Bible's divine authorship is prophecy (used here in its predictive sense). In the Bible God has foretold events in history with such absolute accuracy that there is no way the human mind could have done it. Only the mind of God could have foreseen them.

Only God who knows all could give us, detail by detail, history before it happened. And this is precisely what the Bible does.

Prophecy is a declaration of future events which no human is capable of making because it depends on knowing the innumerable contingencies of human affairs which belong exclusively to the omniscience of God. From its very nature, prophecy must be divine revelation. Prophecy is not merely a good guess. Prophecy is not just conjecture. It is the statement of historical fact that is known only to God.

Some people insist that fulfilled prophecy doesn't prove the Bible is the Word of God, but unfulfilled or wrong prophecies could surely prove that the Bible is *not* the Word of God. The divine standard for prophecy is given to us in Deuteronomy

18: "But the prophet, which shall presume to speak a word in My name, which I have not commanded him to speak, or that shall speak in the name of other gods, even that prophet shall die" (v. 20). God doesn't tolerate false prophets. "And if thou say in thine heart, How shall we know the word which the Lord has not spoken? When a prophet speaks in the name of the Lord, if the thing follow not, nor come to pass, that is the thing which the Lord hath not spoken, but the prophet hath spoken it presumptuously; thou shalt not be afraid of him" (vv. 21-22).

The standard for God's prophets was absolute accuracy. If therefore we find one prophecy in the Bible that didn't come to pass as the Bible said, then we can set aside the Bible as being unreliable by God's own standard.

From the Beginning
Do you know that the first Christian sermon ever preached was based on prophecy? We read in the Book of Acts that Peter stood up before the crowd on the Day of Pentecost and said that God had determined that Christ would die. Immediately he launched into the prophecies of the Book of Psalms as they related to the Messiah. The preaching of the other apostles and of the early church leaders centered frequently on prophetic themes. Fulfilled prophecy has always been a part of Christian preaching.

Prophecy in the Bible covers a very broad area. Some relates to large groups of people; some to individuals; some to rulers; some to cities; some to nations; some to the whole world.

Great portions of the Bible are devoted to prophecy. In the Old Testament, for example, there are 20 consecutive chapters of prophecy in Isaiah, 17 in Jeremiah, 9 in Ezekiel, and 2 in Amos. They predict doom for Ammon, Moab, Edom, Philistia, Babylon, Tyre, and Sidon.

Isaiah sat down one day to write, under the inspiration of

the Holy Spirit, about a man who at that time had not been born: "That saith of Cyrus, He is My shepherd, and shall perform all My pleasure: even saying to Jerusalem, Thou shalt be built; and to the temple, Thy foundation shall be laid" (Isa. 44:28). In modern terms, the prophet might have said, "Folks, a man is coming who is going to release the Jews from captivity and send them back to Jerusalem to build the wall and to build the temple. His name is Cyrus." How could Isaiah say that about Cyrus 150 years before he was born?

"It was a good guess!" you say. Are we to believe that the mother of Cyrus in later years read the prophecy and had a child whom she named Cyrus and whom she brought up to fulfill that prophecy? Not likely. She was a pagan. Surely she had no knowledge of such a prophecy. Neither she nor anyone else could possibly guess that Cyrus was going to be king and release Israel.

Another example of name-before-birth concerned Josiah. "Behold, a child shall be born unto the house of David, Josiah by name; and upon thee shall he offer the priests of the high places that burn incense upon thee, and men's bones shall be burnt upon thee" (1 Kings 13:2). That prophecy was given 300 years before Josiah was born. He was named and it was foretold what he would do. That is exactly how it turned out. No man could have known this in advance. It had to be revealed by God.

God invited people to test the accuracy of His Word. It can stand scrutiny. It has never been wrong. And since it is right, we had better listen to it. Our Lord said, "Take ye heed; behold, I have foretold you all things" (Mark 13:23). He said that in a prophetic context to show us who He is and to call our attention to what He had to say.

The Bible contains many examples of fulfilled prophecy. One concerns the city of Tyre on the Mediterranean Sea. The story is in Ezekiel 26:

Therefore, thus saith the Lord God: Behold, I am against thee, O Tyre, and will cause many nations to come up against thee, as the sea causes its waves to come up. And they shall destroy the walls of Tyre, and break down her towers. I will also scrape her dust from her, and make her like the top of a rock. It shall be a place for the spreading of nets in the midst of the sea; for I have spoken it, saith the Lord God; and it shall become a spoil to the nations (vv. 3-5).

Who is going to do this? A man named Nebuchadnezzar, king of Babylon (v. 7). How he is going to do it?

He shall slay with the sword thy daughters in the field; and he shall make a fort against thee, and cast a mount against thee, and lift up the buckler against thee. And he shall set engines of war against thy walls, and with his axes he shall break down thy towers (vv. 8-9).

What will be the end result of this military action?

And I will make thee like the top of a rock: thou shalt be a place to spread nets upon; thou shalt be built no more; for I the Lord have spoken it, saith the Lord God. . . . I will make thee a terror, and thou shalt be no more; though thou be sought for, yet shalt thou never be found again, saith the Lord God (vv. 14, 21).

Now Tyre wasn't just a little fishing village. It was one of the great cities of Phoenicia. The Phoenicians were the colonizers and mariners of ancient times. They navigated around Africa and established trade routes to the East.

They built themselves a magnificent city with strongly fortified walls 150 feet high and 15 feet thick. The walls protected the land side of the city and navy vessels protected the city from the sea.

Both David and Solomon looked to Tyre for materials and

artisans in their great building projects. The great cedars of Lebanon came through that area. Tyre was important in biblical history as well as secular history.

Three years after Ezekiel had prophesied against Tyre, Nebuchadnezzar came down from the North and did exactly what was predicted. He began a siege of the city and threw up a mound against the city walls. Military tactics back in those days called for cutting off the traffic, trade, supplies, and food to a city, and starving the defenders out. Nebuchadnezzar's siege lasted 13 years. At the end of that time he stormed the city and smashed the walls. He broke down the towers as Ezekiel had predicted. Smashing the towers of a city wasn't always done at the conclusion of a siege, but it was in this case.

When Nebuchadnezzar finally fought his way into the city, he found no spoils because the citizens of Tyre had removed everything of value to a little island one-half mile offshore. There they sat in safety, thumbing their noses at the king of Babylon. Nebuchadnezzar went back home, and the new little community sitting out in the sea flourished for the next 250 years.

Only part of Ezekiel's prophecy had been fulfilled. True, the city had been destroyed and the walls and towers broken down, but what about the stones and timber and dust being thrown into the water? That had not happened.

A young man called Alexander the Great came on the scene. He had defeated the Persians, the second of the world empires foretold by the Prophet Daniel, and was out to conquer the world. He arrived in Phoenician territory with 33,000 infantry, 15,000 cavalry, and a few ships sailing along the coast. He asked the city of Tyre to open its gates to him, but the people refused. They felt secure on their tiny island, which by now had been fortified with a high wall.

Alexander knew that the only way to approach Tyre would be on a land peninsula stretching out to the island. So he set about building a causeway some 200 feet wide stretching out for a half mile.

It was a very difficult task. For material he used what was left of the original city of Tyre. He took the stones and the bricks of the tower and began to toss them into the sea. As the water got deeper and deeper, the project seemed more and more impossible.

To make matters worse, the Tyrians sat on their high walls and bombarded the Greeks with missiles. To protect his operation, Alexander built mobile protection shields. The soldiers and workmen kept these overhead as they moved closer and closer to the island's walls.

Alexander recognized that once he reached the island city he would still have the walls to contend with, so he constructed helepoleis. These were a group of 160-foot-high towers that could be moved on wheels. The idea was to roll these lumbering monsters right out on the causeway and up against the walls, then let down a drawbridge, and march across the top of the wall into the city.

The fact that Alexander was using the rubble of the original city to build his causeway was fulfilling prophecy which said that the site would be scraped bare. What about the prophecy saying that many nations would come against Tyre? As Alexander was building the land bridge, he was being attacked by ships of Tyre on both sides. Alexander saw that he needed ships that could defend his flanks. He went back to the cities and nations he had previously conquered and demanded that they provide him with vessels. He gathered a fleet from Sidon, Byblos, Rhodes, Macedon, and other places. As Ezekiel had said, many nations were coming against Tyre.

Down and Out

At last the causeway to Tyre was complete. Alexander rolled out his big towers and pushed them against the wall. The drawbridges were lowered and the Greek soldiers swarmed into the city. In the battle 18,000 people of Tyre were slain. Another 7,000 were executed, and 30,000 were sold into slavery. The city itself was completely destroyed. This "impossible" victory had been won in seven months. The prophecy of Ezekiel had been fulfilled.

What about the statement that the city would never again be rebuilt? Philip Myers, a historian, wrote, "Alexander the Great reduced Tyre to ruins in 332 B.C. She recovered in a measure, but never to the place she previously held in the world" (*General History for Colleges and High Schools*, Ginn and Company, p. 55). Myers goes on to say that the once great city is now as bare as the top of a rock. It is a place where fishermen dry their nets.

Jerusalem has been rebuilt 17 times, but Tyre has never been rebuilt. Why? Because 25 centuries ago a Jew in Babylon prophesied, "Thou shalt never be rebuilt."

Today the ancient site of Tyre would be an excellent location for a city. It is a beautiful place, well situated, with fresh water to supply a city. But it hasn't been rebuilt, and it won't be.

Do you know what the probability of all the prophecies against Tyre coming true would be? Peter Stoner, a mathematician, figured it as 1 chance in 75 million. Yet, "They all came true in the minutest detail," he wrote in his book *Science Speaks* (Moody Press, p. 80).

All about Nineveh

Nineveh was one of the great cities of the ancient world and the capital of the Assyrian empire. It had a 100-foot-high inner wall that was 50 feet thick. Towers went as high as 200 feet. It had 15 gates and a 150-foot moat. The city was walled in for a 7-mile circumference.

Nineveh had a double wall, the outer wall about 2,000 feet

from the inner wall. To get into the heart of the city, one had to get over the outer wall, go one-half mile, cross a 150-foot moat, and scale a 100-foot wall protected by 200-foot towers. That was quite a fortification. Nineveh, which reached its high point in history in 663 B.C., gave its people a feeling of security.

But anyone who knew Bible prophecy would not have felt safe. The whole Book of Nahum centered on Nineveh:

But with an overrunning flood He will make an utter end of the place thereof, and darkness shall pursue His enemies. What do ye imagine against the Lord? He will make an utter end; affliction shall not rise up the second time. For while they be folden together as thorns, and while they are drunken as drunkards, they shall be devoured as stubble fully dry (Nahum 1:8-10).

So God was going to deal with Nineveh just once. While the people were having their orgies and drunken brawls, the enemy would come in and wipe out the city in one blow. How would all this happen? With an overrunning flood: "The gates of the rivers shall be opened, and the palace shall be dissolved" (Nahum 2:6). Rivers ran through cities in those days. Of course, they had to put an area in the wall where the river would come through, then they would put iron gates through the river, and the water would flow through the gates. But in a flood, the gates would wash away. When there were no gates, there was no protection. History tells us that this is exactly what came to pass. The gates of Nineveh were carried away with a great flood, and the Medes, Babylonians, and Scythians entered the city and took it.

God also said, "There is no healing of thy bruise; thy wound is grievous" (Nahum 3:19). In other words, the city was not to be rebuilt, and it has never been. There is no Nineveh today.

What does all this fulfilled prophecy of the past—and we could give many more examples—mean to us today? It underscores the fact that the Bible is true. If it is true in what it says about Tyre and Nineveh, this provides strong evidence that it is true in what it tells us about Jesus Christ, about sin, about heaven, and hell. As the prophecies of the past have come to pass, so will those of the future. As God has judged people and cities and nations for rejecting Him in the past, so will He judge those who reject Him in the future. It is a warning for the unsaved to get right with God, and for those who are believers to get down to business in serving Him, to bow to the Lordship of Jesus Christ.

The Bible is true.

10
Which
Way
to
God?

The ultimate issue in this whole matter of the Bible comes down to God's wisdom versus man's wisdom (philosophy). We have been looking at many evidences that strongly support the claim that the Bible is God's revelation. In view of all this, why do unregenerate men reject God's revelation and try to explain away the evidences we have touched on in this little volume? The reason is their humanistic philosophy. Human wisdom always sets itself against the Gospel. It wants no part of Christ or the Cross (1 Cor. 1:18—2:16).

Too often man's reasoning gets mixed with revelation, and revelation loses. For example, the Bible teaches that the first five books—Genesis, Exodus, Leviticus, Numbers, and Deuteronomy—were written by Moses. The Jews referred to these books as the Law of Moses. Today we call them the Pentateuch, which means *five*.

More than a century ago, a group of men came along and said, in effect, that only what makes sense to the human intellect is true. They took a look at the Pentateuch and said, "There are things here we can't understand. We don't agree that Moses wrote the first five books because the evolution of legal ethics came much later in history. Moses could not have written the Ten Commandments that early." Thus they concluded that Moses did not write Genesis through Deuteronomy.

Who did? They reasoned something like this: "Well, some men we'll refer to as J, E, D, and P did. You see, whenever the name Jehovah is used for God in the text, that means that the *J* writer was at work. And when the *Elohim* name for God is used, that's a mark of the *E* writer. And we've assigned *D* for the one who wrote Deuteronomy, and *P* for the efforts of the Priestly writer."

One problem with that position is that sometimes the work of *J*, *E*, and *D* show up in the same verse! As for Moses not being able to give the Law, historians have discovered the Code of Hammurabi, a legal system that *predated* Moses.

Out with Creation, In with Evolution

For another example of how human philosophy can nullify revelation, consider the Bible teaching that God is the Creator of all things. In Genesis 1:1 we read, "In the beginning God created the heaven and the earth." On the first day, the second day, the third day, the fourth day, the fifth day, and the sixth day, God created. And on the seventh day, God rested. The Bible is very explicit that God created.

"Oh, no," say some. "The only explanation for our existence is evolution." Evolutionists go on to explain that once upon a time there was a primeval puddle. One writer calls it "pre-biotic soup." And in this primeval puddle was a one-celled thing that was very distressed about being all alone. It wanted company, so it split and became two. Then, of course, everything went wild, and here we are! That is a very limited scientific explanation of evolution. Does the Bible speak of evolution? No, the word doesn't appear in Scripture. Human philosophy speaks of evolution, but the Word of God does not.

Some people can't swallow the puddle story, but neither can they accept the biblical account that God completed all of Creation in six days. So they say, "We believe in theistic evolution. We'll have a conglomerate of both. God made the puddle, and then it evolved until man arrived. At that point God zapped man with a soul." Once again, man's idea imposes itself on revelation, and revelation is the loser. We don't need evolution, and God certainly doesn't need it.

Another illustration is found in the field of psychology. The Bible tells us how to live. It says the way to get rid of guilt is to confess sin. I know of no better way. I can't name one psychiatrist who can deliver anybody from sin. Yet some who are familiar with the Bible go off to universities to study human psychology for several years. Then they try to mix psychology and the Bible, and very often Scripture loses; the Bible is conformed to human thinking.

Others who seem to be working within the framework of religion actually pull the rug out from under biblical Christianity. One example is the German theologian, Rudolph Bultmann. Bultmann tried to "demythologize" Scripture. This means he wanted to take all the "myths" out of the Bible. And what is a *myth*? It was any parts of the Scriptures that Bultmann didn't believe. Bultmann's philosophy imposed on revelation, and again revelation lost.

His or Ours
God's revelation must not be altered by man's adding or subtracting. In the final analysis, there are only two views of life—God's and man's. The man-centered view is unrealistic, panders to the flesh, elevates desire, supports pride, and advocates independence from God. It changes the truth of God into a lie and worships the creature more than the Creator (Rom. 1:25). That is the result of man's view of life.

What is the antithesis of human philosophy? What does God's revelation set forth as man's great need? The central message of the Bible is simple. It declares that man has sinned and that God in the person of Jesus Christ died a sacrificial death on a cross to pay the penalty for the sin of all who acknowledge their need. Those who believe that Christ died on the cross and arose from the grave for them, and who affirm the Lordship of Christ, can have their eternal destiny secured in heaven forever.

Many people who hear that proclamation say the idea is foolish. That is exactly the response predicted in 1 Corinthians 1:18: "For the preaching of the Cross is to them that perish foolishness; but unto us which are saved it is the power of God."

Here again is the great conflict—the word of the Cross versus the word of human wisdom. The word of the Cross in this context means all that is involved in the Cross—the total revelation and work of God. The entire Bible is, in a sense, the preaching of the Cross. All that was written in the Bible before the Cross points to it in anticipation, and everything written after the Cross explains it, points people back to it. Everything that God has to say to us, then, centers around the work of Christ on the cross.

What is the future of human wisdom? The Word of God tells us: "The wisdom of their wise men shall perish, and the understanding of their prudent men shall be hid" (Isa. 29:14). The day is coming when all the philosophies of men shall be swept away, when all of man's wisdom will become ashes. Then Christ alone will reign as King of kings with His believing people.

Jeremiah 8:9 raises a vital issue: "The wise men are ashamed; they are dismayed and taken: lo, they have rejected the Word of the Lord; and what wisdom is in them?" If a person rejects God's revelation, what wisdom is left to him?

None. God is set against such wisdom that leaves Him out. He will destroy it.

This kind of human wisdom is best defined in the Bible in James 3:15: "This wisdom descendeth not from above, but is earthly, sensual, devilish." Such human wisdom is earthly in that it never gets beyond this world; it never really understands divine reality. It is sensual in that it is based on human desire and lust; it is demonic in that its source is Satan, or it helps fulfill Satan's purposes.

What can that kind of wisdom accomplish? Not very much. Throughout history man's wisdom has never solved his eternal problems.

"Wait a minute," someone objects, "we used to be living out in the bush, but now we're residing in condominiums and penthouse suites."

Yes, but we are as sinful now as in the past. Human wisdom has only made us more comfortable in our problems.

What has man's wisdom done to make him nobler, to give him a purer heart? Nothing. The wisdom of this world is a failure when it has to redeem men, when it tries to transform sinners, because it never gets to the real issue of dealing with man's eternal soul. It falls short of what should be its great objective—the knowledge of God. Human philosophy fails to include God, and therefore, never experiences His peace, joy, forgiveness, freedom from guilt, meaning to life, and eternal hope.

God moved in to do what human wisdom could not accomplish: "For after that in the wisdom of God the world by wisdom knew not God, it pleased God by the foolishness of preaching to save them that believe" (1 Cor. 1:21). What man's wisdom could never do, God did through Christ's death on the cross. The way it becomes effective in our lives is through belief in what Christ accomplished for us as revealed in His Word—the Bible.

Hard to Get a Conviction

Not all who claim to be Christians, however, believe that the Bible is without error, completely infallible in every detail and singularly authoritative. Among many so-called Christians there is a lack of conviction about the Scripture. In his book *God Has Spoken*, J.I. Packer comments on this.

Certainty about the great issues of Christian faith and conduct is lacking all along the line. The outside observer sees us as staggering on from gimmick to gimmick and stunt to stunt like so many drunks in a fog, not knowing at all where we are or which way we should be going. Preaching is hazy; heads are muddled; hearts fret; doubts drain our strength; uncertainty paralyzes action. We know the Victorian shibboleth that to travel hopefully is better than to arrive, and it leaves us cold. Ecclesiastics of a certain type tell us that the wish to be certain is mere weakness of the flesh, a sign of spiritual immaturity, but we do not find ourselves able to believe them. We know in our bones that we were made for certainty, and we cannot be happy without it. Yet, unlike the first Christians who in three centuries won the Roman world, and those later Christians who pioneered the Reformation, and the Puritan awakening, and the Evangelical revival, and the great missionary movement of the last century, we lack certainty. Why is this? We blame the external pressures of modern secularism, but this is like Eve blaming the serpent. The real trouble is not in our circumstances, but in ourselves (Revell, pp. 11-12).

How tragic! Man has decided that his own intellectualism is the answer to everything. Our Christian society has become a swirl of self-centered deciders who themselves want to determine truth.

The result is that the Word of God is diminished or lost. The Prophet Amos spoke of a similar scene: "Behold, the days come, saith the Lord God, that I will send a famine in the land, not a famine of bread, nor a thirst for water, but of hearing the words of the Lord" (Amos 8:11).

Amos goes on to describe the spiritual destitution that results when we don't love the Word of the Lord. He pictures frantic souls wandering everywhere, listening with hopes of hearing God's voice—but never hearing it (v. 12).

In recent years God's Word had lost in the church to liberalism, denominationalism, programism, and social activity, but that is changing. There is a new thrust of Bible study and teaching. Christians are again renewing the age-old orthodox view of Scripture.

This book is written with the prayer that it will be one of many catalysts to end the famine of the Word and stimulate the confidence of God's people in God's matchless Book—the Bible, and even lead someone to the Saviour, the Lord Jesus Christ.